Long
Night's
Journey
into Day

San Diego Christian College
2100 Greenfield Drive
El Cajon, CA 92019

D0311508

ALSO BY JAMES EMERY WHITE

Rethinking the Church
A Search for the Spiritual
You Can Experience a Spiritual Life
You Can Experience a Purposeful Life
You Can Experience an Authentic Life
Life-Defining Moments

241.3
W585ℓ

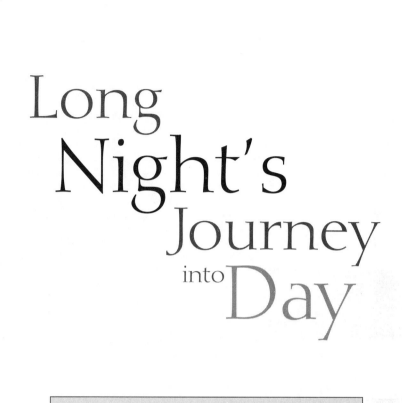

Long Night's Journey into Day

The Path *Away* from Sin

JAMES EMERY WHITE

WaterBrook
PRESS

LONG NIGHT'S JOURNEY INTO DAY
PUBLISHED BY WATERBROOK PRESS
2375 Telstar Drive, Suite 160
Colorado Springs, Colorado 80920
A division of Random House, Inc.

All Scripture quotations, unless otherwise indicated, are taken from the *Holy Bible, New International Version*®. NIV®. Copyright © 1973, 1978, 1984 by International Bible Society. Used by permission of Zondervan Publishing House. All rights reserved. Scripture quotations marked (TLB) are taken from *The Living Bible* copyright © 1971. Used by permission of Tyndale House Publishers, Inc., Wheaton, Illinois 60189. All rights reserved. Scripture quotations marked (NLT) are taken from *The Holy Bible, New Living Translation,* copyright © 1996. Used by permission of Tyndale House Publishers, Inc., Wheaton, Illinois 60189. All rights reserved. Scripture quotations marked (MSG) are taken from *The Message.* Copyright © by Eugene H. Peterson 1993, 1994, 1995. Used by permission of NavPress Publishing Group. Scripture quotations marked (NCV) are taken from *The Holy Bible, New Century Version* (NCV), copyright © 1987, 1988, 1991 by Word Publishing, Nashville, TN 37214. Used by permission. Scripture quotations marked (RSV) are taken from the *Revised Standard Version of the Bible,* copyright © 1946, 1952, and 1971 by the Division of Christian Education of the National Council of the Churches of Christ in the USA. Used by permission. Scripture quotations marked (NKJV) are taken from the *New King James Version.* Copyright © 1982 by Thomas Nelson, Inc. Used by permission. All rights reserved. Scripture quotations marked (CEV) are from the *Contemporary English Version.* Copyright © 1991, 1992, 1995 by American Bible Society. Used by permission. Scripture quotations marked (Phillips) are taken from *The New Testament in Modern English, Revised Edition* © 1972 by J. B. Phillips. Scripture quotations marked (TEV) are from the *Today's English Version*—Second Edition. Copyright © 1992 by American Bible Society. Used by permission. Scripture quotations marked (NASB) are taken from the *New American Standard Bible*®. © Copyright The Lockman Foundation 1960, 1962, 1963, 1968, 1971, 1972, 1973, 1975, 1977. Used by permission. (www.Lockman.org).

ISBN 1-57856-455-7

Copyright © 2002 by James Emery White

All rights reserved. No part of this book may be reproduced or transmitted in any form or by any means, electronic or mechanical, including photocopying and recording, or by any information storage and retrieval system, without permission in writing from the publisher.

WATERBROOK and its deer design logo are registered trademarks of WaterBrook Press, a division of Random House, Inc.

Library of Congress Cataloging-in-Publication Data
White, James Emery, 1961-
   Long night's journey into day : the path away from sin / James Emery White.
     p. cm.
Includes bibliographical references.
   ISBN 1-57856-455-7
   1. Christian life. 2. Deadly sins. 3. Virtues. I. Title.
   BV4509.5 .W4542 2002
   241'.3—dc21

                                                                2002004936

Printed in the United States of America
2002—First Edition

10 9 8 7 6 5 4 3 2 1

Contents

Contents

Acknowledgments

Though she is better known for such literary characters as Lord Peter Wimsey, the insightful Dorothy Sayers (1893–1957) is, in many ways, the inspiration for this book. Her wonderful little essay "The Other Six Deadly Sins," from *Creed or Chaos,* introduced me to what could be gained by exploring the ancient listing of the deadly sins for one's own struggle with sin and the journey to become more like Christ through the power of the Holy Spirit.

I am again indebted to my assistant, Ms. Glynn Goble, who does nothing less than free me to fulfill God's calling on my life and who daily reminds me of what a life that has been truly transformed by Christ actually looks like.

My vocation as a pastor remains intact through the good humor of the community of faith known as Mecklenburg Community Church. I cannot imagine serving anywhere else, or ever wanting to.

This book marks a second venture in a publishing partnership with WaterBrook Press, a division of Random House, Inc. Thanks goes to Ron Lee, who, along with his team, is the most maddeningly meticulous editor as to sources and permissions I have ever worked with (which means he is very good and lets me get by with very little), and Kirsten Blomquist, who takes the book and gets the word out about it. Thanks to you both.

As always, the greatest thanks goes to my wife, Susan, who makes every page possible.

Keep me from the death of deadly sin which puts hell in my soul. Keep me from the murder of lust that blinds and poisons my heart.... Keep me from loving money in which is hatred, from avarice and ambition that suffocate my life.... Stanch in me the rank wound of covetousness and the hungers that exhaust my nature with the bleeding. Stamp out the serpent envy that stings love with poison and kills all joy.... Untie my hands and deliver my heart from sloth. Set me free from the laziness that goes about disguised as activity when activity is not required of me, and from the cowardice that does what is not demanded, in order to escape sacrifice.... But give me the strength that waits upon You in silence and peace. Give me humility in which alone is rest, and deliver me from pride which is the heaviest of burdens. And possess my whole heart and soul with the simplicity of love...for You alone.[1]

A prayer by Thomas Merton

The Journey of Transformation

Three Essential Dynamics of Lasting Soul Development

American playwright Eugene O'Neill asked that his highly autobiographical play *A Long Day's Journey into Night* not be published until all of the principal parties who are portrayed in the work were no longer living. Since O'Neill's parents and siblings, the inspiration for the play's main characters, had died years earlier, the playwright's wife allowed the work to be published in 1956.

The tale of the Tyrones—the fictional name for the O'Neill family—is not a happy one. The youngest son is dispatched to a sanitarium for treatment of a chronic physical illness, despising the father who sent him there. The mother is addicted to narcotics, the older brother to alcohol. Blame is freely passed while misery rules. The family talks openly of their problems, and they jointly curse the darkness, but the darkness never recedes. The life of this family was, indeed, a long day's journey into night.

1

Contrast O'Neill's tragic tale with the Christian journey. The life of faith, rather than presenting a long day's journey into night, is in fact a long night's journey into day. Yes, life is dark. But the promise and hope that are brought to us through Christ is that of light—not in the temporary, superficial sense of personal peace and comfort, but in the profound sense of a life freed from its soul-binding chains and infused with the power of the living God. The Christian life enables us to become what we were created to be.

If this is really true, however, why aren't we experiencing this dramatic transformation? In other words, why aren't Christians becoming more like Christ?

Author and former pastor Eugene Peterson reflects on attending a religious conference as an adolescent. People from his church gathered every summer by a lake, where they exhibited fiery spiritual intensity and parroted phrases like "experiencing the deeper life" and receiving "a second blessing" from God. Yet as the young Peterson observed the lives of his fellow parishioners, he noticed little continuity between the exuberance they expressed at the conference grounds and their everyday life back in town. "The mothers of our friends who were bitchy before," he notes, "were bitchy still."[1]

This lack of change certainly is not the sole province of self-satisfied Christians. Bill Phillips, a fitness guru and the author of the bestseller *Body for Life,* tells about attending a fitness convention and coming face-to-face with a number of his readers. They were happy to see him, but he wasn't so happy to see *them.*

These fans had been reading Phillips's books and getting his fitness magazine for years, but of the six hundred people he encountered, only about eighty looked like they were physically fit. The other five hundred—who had access to the very same information on fitness and health—looked like they'd never even heard of exercise, much less had any firsthand exposure to it. Something had broken down on the road to *experience*.[2]

These out-of-shape followers of Bill Phillips had lost their way on the transformational journey. It's easy to do if you're unaware of the three dynamics that are essential to personal transformation, whether it's spiritual or physical. These three dynamics are desire, knowledge, and power. Desire is the longing for change, knowledge is the awareness of the path you need to take to experience change, and power is the ability to capitalize on your desire and knowledge. Most Christians have enormous desire for God and the things of God. They sincerely want to be like Christ and have their lives ordered around His will. The breakdown comes later, with knowledge and power.

TRANSFORMATION AT A CROSSROADS

How can Christians join their desire for life transformation with the knowledge and power required to make it happen? It begins with a new understanding of knowledge. The biblical idea of knowledge is alien to most people today, since it has little to do with brain function or mental awareness. In the Bible, to know was the same as to do. To believe was to behave. Biblical knowledge, by its very nature, is transformational since it requires action and leads to change.

This approach to knowledge is very different from our modern understanding, which associates knowledge with the acquisition of information. But having a grasp of information is never enough to produce meaningful life-change. This helps explain why Christians who are familiar with the basic principles of the faith still struggle in regard to spirituality. They

3

understand the concept of God the Father; they simply don't know how to relate to Him or how to become more like His Son. They have the right information, but they need the knowledge that leads to experiencing God and His power in a personal way. If we confuse knowledge with information, we'll get sidetracked on the journey of personal transformation. We need to grasp the Bible's view of knowledge: To know truly is to do, and to do is the first step in becoming the person we desire to become. Knowledge is action, and the right actions lead to personal transformation.

But the biblical practice of knowledge alone won't produce lasting life-change. We need to add the final dynamic essential to personal transformation, which is power. It is the greatest of ironies that any Christian would be lacking in power, but we are. Being a Christian means we have been filled with God's power through the indwelling of the Holy Spirit. The power within us is the same power that raised Jesus from the dead. Clearly the problem is not one of access to sufficient power. Instead, it's our inability—or unwillingness—to open the most critical parts of who we are to the transforming energies of the Holy Spirit. As long as we close ourselves to the exercise of God's power, we'll miss out on personal transformation.

The basic dynamic of spiritual transformation is found at the intersection of knowledge and power. It is knowingly bringing the power of God to bear on the critical issues of soul development. Anything less than complete openness to the work of God in our lives, through the operation of His power, will fail to bring about a transformed life.

Imagine discovering a sore on your arm. You immediately apply a general, topical antiseptic and wait for healing. But what if the sore is the result of skin cancer? The surface treatment will not address the issue. Not only will new lesions appear, but the cancer will continue to spread internally.

The Bible teaches that just such a cancer is infecting our souls, and that cancer is sin—the deepest problem facing human existence. This interior life is the area that we need to open fully to God and His power.

DENYING THE PROBLEM

If we suffered from cancer, we'd do whatever was necessary to be healed of its ravages. So why do we hesitate to seek God's treatment for the spiritual cancer of sin? Part of the answer lies in our culture's discomfort with the direct acknowledgement of this destructive force.

The fields of psychology and sociology, observes essayist and social critic Henry Fairlie, "shirk the problem of evil." These disciplines contend that "our…faults and those of our societies are the result of some kind of mechanical failure, which has only to be diagnosed and understood for us to set it right."[3] Psychologist Karl Menninger painstakingly detailed our collective loss of any sense of personal wrongdoing in his provocatively titled work *Whatever Became of Sin?*, which details how the theological notion of sin became the legal idea of crime and then slid further from its true meaning when it was relegated to the psychological category of sickness.[4]

The slide continues today, at the beginning of the twenty-first century. Sin is now regarded as little more than a set of emotions that can be explained through genetics. Lust is not a wrong that threatens our own health and the well-being of others; it's simply an emotional urge that is rooted in the need to propagate the human species. It's fixed in our genes. One molecular biologist even referred to Dante's description of the descent into hell as the journey into the "genetic inferno," reducing sin to nothing more than a series of chemical reactions independent of a moral will.[5]

While the concept of sin continues to be explained away, the greatest reduction of evil is to dismiss it altogether, turning vice into a morally neutral matter of personal choice. Some even twist evil so completely that they make it an aspect of virtue. Thus lust becomes "sensuality," greed becomes "resource management optimization," and anger "being honest with your emotions." Pride, of course, is little more than "asserting your self-worth," and envy is that which fuels "the spirit of healthy competition."[6] Dorothy Sayers ruthlessly exposes this semantic sleight of hand by noting that a person "may be greedy and selfish; spiteful, cruel, jealous, and unjust; violent and brutal; grasping, unscrupulous, and a liar; stubborn and arrogant; stupid, morose, and dead to every noble instinct—and still we are ready to say of him that he is not an immoral man."[7]

No matter how we try to talk our way around it, life has a way of bringing us back to sin's reality and our need to confront it. In his book *Explaining Hitler,* Ron Rosenbaum surveys theory after theory regarding the Nazi leader's atrocities. In the end, all of his explanations fail to confront the "laughing" Hitler, the bloodthirsty dictator who was fully conscious of his malignancy. He didn't have to kill the Jews; he wasn't compelled by abstract forces. In truth, he chose to, he *wanted* to. Here was simply an evil man.[8]

But so are we all.

No, we don't like the word *evil,* especially when it is applied to our own character. It seems preposterous to lump ourselves in with the evil company of a butcher like Hitler, but we too make choices—and many of them are not of God. It remains an inescapable truth that evil manifests itself in our everyday life as a result of our willful determination to embrace it. We keep it a secret, attempting to ensure that only we know where, and how deeply, it has taken root in us.[9] But evil is firmly established within us. As Mark Twain wrote, "Man is the only animal that blushes. Or needs to."[10]

The great souls of the past didn't deny this reality. Instead, they embraced it. C. S. Lewis commented that some readers paid him an unexpected compliment in regard to the writing of *The Screwtape Letters,* the fictitious account of one demon's counsel to a younger demon on the intricacies of successful temptation. The readers presumed that Lewis's reflections were the ripe fruit of many years' study in moral and ascetic theology. "They forgot that there is an equally reliable...way of learning how temptation works," Lewis wrote. " 'My heart'—I need no other's—'showeth me the wickedness of the ungodly.' "[11] Lewis's admission reflects the great insight into soul development that is found in the teaching of the apostle John: "If we claim to be without sin, we deceive ourselves and the truth is not in us."[12] When we refuse to acknowledge the reality of our sin, we become what M. Scott Peck calls "people of the lie."[13]

We try to cover over our evil, yet few can live in such denial. A Web site designed to gather anonymous confessions from around the world as a dumping ground for sin astounded even its creators. Thousands upon thousands flocked to this Internet "altar" to confess their wrongdoings. The candor found on its pages is arresting:

> "i love my body! i swear i really do. im 5'9", 105 lbs. long
> blonde hair and really tan! i always say o no im not pretty, or o
> no im not skinny when ppl comment on my looks, but you
> know what I wanna say one day, YES I KNOW I AM SKIN-
> NIER AND CUTER THAN YOU AND I LOVE IT!!! i just
> love my body, love it...."

> "I've hit snooze 5 consecutive times. Each alarm is 9 minutes
> apart. I get out of bed 45 minutes later than I should and end
> up at work late."

"I've been to rehab twice and just went through detox again. And I still plan on shooting up later."

"I am so jealous of people that have enough money to do what they want. I want money, money, money! I am tired of going 'without'. I know I should be grateful for what I have, but I want MORE!!!!"

"I'm married and I have had 5 affairs in 11 yrs."[14]

THE BLINDNESS OF SELF-DECEIT

A careful diagnosis of this universal problem brings us back to sin. Not just any sin, but *our* sin—the errant acts and thoughts, words and deeds that plague our lives. It's this sin that must be confronted and exposed to the light of day. Labeling sin accurately and recognizing it in ourselves is the knowledge we must gain in order to have the deepest parts of who we are exposed to the transforming power of God.

Yet we live in a world where we see only what we want to see, hear only what we want to hear, and read only what we want to read. Through the technology of cyberspace, we have the ability to filter out everything but what we wish to be exposed to—creating what University of Chicago professor Cass Sunstein calls the "Daily Me." This is a self-created world in which we see only the sports highlights that concern our favorite team, read only the issues that address our interests, and engage only the op-ed pieces with which we agree. The highly lauded personalization of information protects us from exposure to anything that might challenge our thinking or make us uncomfortable. We begin to follow the sound of nothing more than the echo of our own voice.[15]

Sunstein only concerns himself with the implications this holds for democracy. But the far deeper issue is its effect on our souls. When it comes to our spiritual lives, we need an outside voice—something ruthlessly unfiltered—that will accurately address the state of our inner world. We need a reminder from the prophet Jeremiah: "The heart is deceitful above all things."[16] Apart from this knowledge, the power of God can't be unleashed. Just as light becomes more powerful as it is brought into focus, so the power of God is optimized as we focus the light of truth and use it to peer into the darkness of our soul. Apart from this light, there is only blinding self-deceit. We become worse than the people Mark Twain described: We're the ones who need to blush but no longer know how to.

Many are now familiar with the story of Robert Philip Hanssen, the former FBI counterintelligence agent who pled guilty to spying for Moscow. Hanssen caused the worst intelligence breach in U.S. history. The irony is that this self-confessed traitor considered himself to be a devout Christian. Throughout his twenty-five-year FBI career, Hanssen would tell friends and colleagues that without religion, men were lost. When FBI agents held going-away parties at strip clubs near the bureau's headquarters, Hanssen refused to attend, saying it would be a sin.

When he was arrested on charges that he'd been spying since 1985—first for the Soviet Union, and then after the Soviet collapse, for Russia—those who knew him were stunned. His closest friends and colleagues said they could only offer a guess as to why a man who seemed to possess such strong Christian faith would have engaged in anti-American espionage.

They speculated that he "must have been able to compartmentalize his life, deluding himself into thinking that espionage was simply an exciting intellectual challenge that had nothing to do with leading a good, moral Christian life."[17]

AN ANCIENT SOLUTION

The ancients understood such behavior. To compartmentalize one's life, isolating faith and morals from certain behaviors, was identified as self-deception. To address this condition, the early church formulated a short list of sins that could be used to confront the delusion of sin. The original list contained eight sins: pride, envy, anger, laziness, greed, gluttony, lust, and sadness.[18] The idea was not that these represented the most despicable sins imaginable, but rather that they were the root from which all other sins established themselves.[19] If this small grouping of sins could be engaged, then one could address the entire playing field of sin and be set free to pursue the counterpart virtues of the eight deadliest sins. A person could move from pride to humility, envy to a sense of security, anger to restraint, laziness to persistence and diligence, greed to contentment, gluttony to moderation, lust to self-control, and sadness to joy. It was life on the other side of sin, the completed journey from night into day, that gave the ancient list its great worth. The church fathers understood, as theologian Cornelius Plantinga has noted, that "God hates sin not just because it violates his law but, more substantively,…because it interferes with the way things are supposed to be."[20]

The deadly sins were first identified as a group within the cloisters of the early monastic movement of the Eastern Church. Because the monastic life focused so intensely on the inner self and spirituality, it's not surprising that a deep understanding of our sinful nature evolved there.[21] Men and women who devoted themselves to the rigors of actual transformation, seeking to reform the depths of the human heart, began to see certain sins as the foundation of all challenges.

Evagrius of Pontus (346–399), often cited as "the great architect of the contemplative way," is noted as the first compiler.[22] His list included gluttony, fornication, avarice, dejection (or "lack of pleasure"), anger, weariness, vainglory, and pride.[23] The list entered the West in the fourth century through John Cassian of Marseilles, who in all likelihood met Evagrius during a visit to Egypt.[24] During the sixth century, Pope Gregory the Great modified the grouping into a defined list of seven. Of the original eight fashioned by Evagrius and put forward by Cassian, Gregory's listing folded vainglory into pride, and weariness into sadness. Then Gregory added envy. His goal was to so define the sins that they were "able to serve as a classification of the normal perils of the soul in the ordinary conditions of life."[25] The church soon substituted the seemingly vague sin of sadness with the more specific sin of sloth, and the list became known as the seven deadly sins.

Throughout the Middle Ages, the seven deadly sins were kept before church worshipers and the general public through literature and through required readings of the list before assembled congregations.[26] But then the warning voice of the deadly sins was drowned out during the Renaissance and fell on deaf ears during the humanism of the Enlightenment. For the preceding one thousand years they had served the greatest of souls and keenest of minds as they brought desire, knowledge, and power together for the journey of personal transformation from night into day. Now they were largely silenced by man's reliance on the supposed inherent goodness of humanity.

DUSTING OFF THE LIST

It's time to return to the ancient wisdom and insights of the deadly sins and their counterpart virtues. As theologian Simon Chan notes, it is only through such an enterprise that we are able to "put names to the sins and recognize them for what they are."[27] This is particularly critical in our day, when the force and full meaning of these sins are increasingly foreign. We are like the residents of Macondo in Gabriel Garcia Marquez's *One Hundred Years of Solitude,* who, due to their isolation, had to put labels on things like chairs, hammers, and tables in order to not forget the names that went with them. Likewise, due to our culture's failure to put truth and morality into the mainstream, we must run quickly and put labels to what earlier generations knew how to name. If we fail, we may lose the language altogether.[28]

Chan goes on to remind us that "in real life we need to deal with specific sins, besetting sins, often one overpowering sin that dogs us throughout life."[29] Scripture shares this sentiment, encouraging us in its own list-specific way to "put to death, therefore, whatever belongs to your earthly nature: sexual immorality, impurity, lust, evil desires and greed, which is idolatry.... You must rid yourselves of all such things as these: anger, rage, malice, slander, and filthy language."[30]

It is only in allowing evil to be named by a higher authority than ourselves that we can hear a voice that comes from beyond the "Daily Me." It is only by taking this ancient list of sins seriously that we can open ourselves to the transforming power of God. A careful consideration of the deadly sins, eight in number when we reference the earliest list, will open us to the three essential dynamics of personal transformation: desire, knowledge, and power.[31] We long for authentic life-change, and we get there by identifying the sins and then drawing on God's power to practice their counterpart virtues. The church fathers knew this. We can know it as well.

The Path Away from Sin

Joining with God for the Journey

Every day, approximately one hundred prison inmates are released into the streets of Huntsville, Texas. Though there are fifty-eight prisons holding more than 130,000 inmates in the state, male prisoners are always released from the prison system's state headquarters at the Huntsville unit.

Former inmates emerge from a gate in the red brick walls wearing ill-fitting lime-green short-sleeved shirts and bearing laundry bags stuffed with personal belongings. Each man is given an outfit of cheap clothes, a check for fifty dollars, and a state voucher good for one bus ticket out of town. With no one to greet them, most of the men stream past the private homes and prison offices toward the Greyhound station three blocks away. They cash their checks in a nearby store, buy new clothes, and then board a bus to take them away.

Are they free? Yes. Have they been given a new lease on life? Without question. But ahead of each of these men lies a perilous journey. Positioned to greet them as they board the bus is a welcoming committee of prostitutes and drug dealers whose only goal is to ensnare them in their previous way of living.[1]

Welcome to a sobering picture of the new life in Christ. When you commit yourself to Christ, you immediately become a new creation. You've left the prison of your old nature, and you've taken on a new identity, defined by your relationship with God through Christ. The power of sin to rule your life has been broken, destroyed by the cross of Christ. And you have been raised with Christ into newness of life. A completely fresh life awaits you.

Are you free? Yes. Have you been given a new lease on life? Without question. But as C. S. Lewis's fictitious demon Screwtape counsels his young nephew Wormwood on the intricacies of temptation after his "patient" becomes a Christian, "All the habits of the patient, both mental and bodily, are still in our favour."[2] The interplay between our freedom from the power of sin and our freedom to still commit sin is one of the most perplexing dynamics related to the spiritual life. Understanding that interplay lies at the heart of joining with God for the transformational journey.

THE SAINTS WE ARE

One of the most sweeping and dramatic declarations in Scripture is that every Christian is a saint. Not *will be* or *might be,* but *is.* Consider the prominence of this assertion, found six times in the New Testament book of Ephesians. Paul begins by writing: "Paul, an apostle of Christ Jesus by the will of God, To the *saints* in Ephesus."[3]

With that as an introduction, he continues: "So then you are no longer strangers and sojourners, but you are fellow citizens with the *saints* and members of the household of God."[4] Then Paul, in talking about himself in relation to other Christians, says, "I am the very least of all the *saints*."[5]

Finally, in closing out the letter, notice how Paul reminds his readers to keep praying for each other: "always keep on praying for all the *saints*."[6]

There is no doubt in Paul's mind about the identity of someone who is in a relationship with Christ. That person is a saint.[7] But surely Paul jests. Saints are supposed to be holy, almost perfect people who have devoted their lives to doing the work of God. They are humble souls who persevere despite great persecution. They lead exemplary lives of service and righteousness. Not many of us fit that description, so what does the Bible mean when it calls someone a saint, especially since it calls *all* Christians saints?

The answer is found in the definition of the word *saint,* which means "those who are set apart." The moment you commit your life to Christ, confess your sins, and repent—putting your trust in Christ as your Forgiver and Leader—something dramatic happens to your spiritual position. The Bible says you were once dead, but now you're alive. You were far off from God, and now you're brought near. You were a stranger to God, and now you're His son or daughter. You were an alien, and now you're a citizen of God's kingdom. In short, you were lost, and now you're found.

No matter who you are, how you have lived, or what you have done, when you come to Christ for forgiveness and enter into a relationship with God, you experience a dramatic identity change. God declares you to be set apart. Your sins have been forgiven. You've been accepted into God's family. In essence, He has said, "You are no longer what you were, or who you were. Because of your acceptance of what Christ did on the cross for you, your sin, your rebellion, your mistakes, your failures, *will not be* the last word, much less the defining reality of your life. As far as I am concerned, you are a new creation. You are holy. You are a saint."

I read of a Christian professor of sociology who was teaching a class called "Social Problems" at the University of Pennsylvania. He often tried to make natural use of the course material to stimulate his students' thinking on spiritual matters. During one class, when dealing with the social problem of the world's oldest profession, he asked, "Have you ever considered what the various religious leaders of the world throughout history would have said to a prostitute?" He asked what Buddha might have said, and what Muhammad's thoughts might have been. He raised the question of what the Mosaic Law had to say about this dehumanizing practice. The discussion became lively and intense.

When the time was ripe, he asked, "What do you suppose Jesus would have said to a prostitute?"

A student on the front row raised his hand and said, "Jesus never met a prostitute."

Sensing his opportunity, the professor said, "Yes, He did. I'll show you in my Bible where—" Just as he was about to "whip the Word" on the young man, the student interrupted him. "You didn't hear me. I said Jesus never met a prostitute."

Once again the professor protested, reached for his New Testament, and began leafing through the pages.

Once again, the student spoke out. "You're not listening to me. I am saying that Jesus never met a prostitute. Do you think that when He looked at Mary Magdalene He saw a prostitute? Do you think He saw whores when he looked at women like her? Jesus never met a prostitute!"

The professor fell silent, dumbfounded by the student's insight. He was absolutely right! Jesus never met a prostitute; He didn't look at people that way.[8] What Jesus saw in Mary Magdalene, and what He sees in you, is someone He loves who has been stained by sin and rebellion. But rather than the sin and rebellion driving Him away, it drove Him to the cross so the stain could be removed and you could be white as snow. In other words, a saint.

THE SAINTS WE'RE BECOMING

But there's more to the identity that awaits us in Christ than merely being declared by God to be a saint *positionally.* He also wants to develop us into saints *functionally.*

When you become a Christian, God has a very clear agenda for your life. It is to make you like Jesus. It is to have you become the person He has already declared you to be. As God announced through the prophet Ezekiel, "I will give you a new heart and put a new spirit in you; I will remove from you your heart of stone and give you a heart of flesh."[9] C. S. Lewis once reflected that we tend to think God simply wants obedience to a set of rules, when in truth He wants people of a particular sort.[10] It's as if God says, "You are a saint, now live like one!" But that's not all. He also says, "And I'll help."

So while sanctification, the gradual process of becoming holy, is "God's gift before it is our goal," it still remains a goal.[11] We are meant to pursue God's promise of moral transformation through the indwelling power and presence of the Holy Spirit until it becomes our daily experience. This is why the writer of Hebrews speaks of striving for holiness.[12]

Imagine that Phil Jackson, who coached the Chicago Bulls and then the Los Angeles Lakers to NBA championships, came to you and said, "You've made the squad. You're now officially a member of a world champion basketball team. Here's your uniform, your locker, everything. And don't worry; your place on the roster has nothing to do with your basketball ability. I'm just choosing to accept you, to bestow upon you this identity. But here's what I want to do: Now that you're on an NBA team, I want you to let me develop you into a professional-level player."

This process of transformation is the great enterprise of God. But how is it going to happen? Not the way you might think, for when it comes to life-change, there are five lies that prevent us from submitting to God's transforming work in our lives.

Lie No. 1: It's All About Knowing

Our culture prizes access to information above just about any other value. We equate knowledge with power and assume that information is what bestows knowledge. When it comes to genuine life-change, this devotion to knowledge is a lie that prevents personal transformation.

It's easy to see why we might fall prey to this lie. From the colonial times to the present, information has dramatically reshaped our nation and the world. Beginning with the postal system and roads of the eighteenth century (and the newspapers, books, and pamphlets they carried), the telegraph and telephone of the nineteenth century, followed by the television, computers, and Internet of the twentieth century, it has been information that has transformed our world socially, economically, and politically.[13] As a result, we tend to believe that the way to solve a problem is to gain more knowledge about it.

Actually, this lie contains a partial truth. If we had the ancient biblical understanding of knowledge, we would indeed be starting the journey of personal transformation. The biblical idea of "knowing" was coupled with doing, and it was intensely personal. There was no separation between true knowledge and life application. To have true knowledge of God was to be in relationship with Him and by extension, to have one's personal conduct correspond to that relationship.[14] For example, the oft-quoted line from Psalms "Be still, and know that I am God" was far from a call to quiet contemplation.[15] It was the command to abandon rebellion in recognition of God's rule. Thus Jesus' distressing forecast of the day when He would be forced to say of false believers, "I never knew you," is more accurately rendered "I never had anything to do with you."[16] Similarly, Paul's declaration that Christ "knew no sin" did not mean that Jesus had no intellectual knowledge of sin, but that He had no personal experience with committing sin.[17] The idea of knowing was inextricably intertwined with the idea of doing and, more important, with being. The apostle James ridiculed the idea of the effectiveness of mere information by writing, "You believe that there is one God. Good! Even the demons believe that."[18]

The truth is that while life-change often begins with information, and knowledge in its fullest and most biblical sense is at the heart of transformation, change does not come from merely learning about the issue at hand. It comes from *taking* the issue in hand. That's the biblical understanding and practice of knowledge.

Lie No. 2: I Have to Change Before I Can Experience God's Power

A second lie has to do with our own role in life-change. When it comes to experiencing the power of God, we tend to feel we need to change first, before we can come to God. We believe that only after we've mustered a certain amount of transformation on our own can we connect with God.

This is what the lie looks like:

> LIFE-CHANGE ————————▶ GOD'S PRESENCE AND POWER

In other words, we believe that our success at changing our own lives somehow leads to an experience of God and His power. It's a lie that sends us into a vicious, self-defeating cycle. We avoid coming to God for help because we don't yet have our lives in order. But when we try to get our lives in order apart from God, we find that we can't, so we never come to God for help. The lie causes us to miss out on life-change because we rank our own efforts ahead of God's.

Here is the accurate, biblical picture:

> GOD'S PRESENCE AND POWER ————————▶ LIFE-CHANGE

The truth is that personal transformation is an activity of God that flows out of a relationship with Him. Life-change begins not with our own efforts but in our relationship with God, and then through that relationship we begin the great journey toward personal transformation. Coming to Christ begins the process.

Lie No. 3: Real Life-Change Happens All at Once, and Is Once for All

Even those who believe the truth that real life-change is a product of God's power often miss the full truth by believing a third lie. We expect God to change our lives all at once and be done with it. This is a terribly truncated view of the miraculous nature of God's work in a human life.

I once read a story about an Eastern king who asked one of his counselors to give him a sign of the miraculous works of God. The counselor told the king to plant four acorns. The king did, but then fell asleep for eighty years. When he awoke and saw that the acorns he had planted had *instantaneously* become four fully grown trees, he thought a miracle had taken place. To him, it seemed like only a moment. The counselor then told the king that, in truth, eighty years had gone by.

The king looked down and saw that he had grown old and that his clothes were in rags. He said, "Then there is no miracle here."

"That is where you are wrong," the counselor replied. "Whether accomplished in a moment or in eighty years, it is all God's work. The miracle is not in the speed of its happening, but in the happening itself."[19]

Deep life-change doesn't often happen the moment your relationship with God begins. The Holy Spirit can do whatever He wishes, of course, but He seldom transforms us instantaneously. When you begin your relationship with God, your eternal destiny is altered, there is a radical reorientation of priorities, there is a new life purpose, and there is the power and work of God in your life. But rather than the instant liberation from every bad habit or character flaw you've ever possessed, what takes place is more like the landing of an army on a beachhead. The battle has begun, but it will take time before the war is won.

This is why the apostle Paul wrote to the Colossians to "Let your roots grow down into him and draw up nourishment from him. See that you go on growing in the Lord, and become strong and vigorous in the truth you were taught."[20] The language in that verse is critical. You have to *let* your roots grow; you have to *draw* up nourishment; you have to *keep on* growing; you have to *become* strong and vigorous. It isn't something that just happens while you stand aside and watch. It's not simply an event, but a process. And even as the process unfolds, it can often reflect a "three steps forward, two steps back, three steps forward" dynamic.[21]

Lie No. 4: The Real Issue Is Sin Management

Is sin best attacked frontally, by battling each thing that doesn't honor God? Or should we focus on holy living, the opposite of sin, in order to rob sin of its power? Dallas Willard describes the difference between these two approaches, calling this lie "sin management."[22] Instead of becoming more like Jesus by practicing holy living, our goal becomes just the opposite: the minimization of the frequency of sin. Instead of focusing on Christ, we concentrate on the sin itself and work harder at keeping it contained. By practicing sin management, we hope that somehow life-change will creep in.

In truth, seeking to avoid sin and asking for forgiveness when we slip up breeds little in the way of transformation. More important, it falls far short of Christ's vision for our lives. I can seek forgiveness on the heels of every materialistic act, but such contrition will fail to address my ongoing struggle with greed. I can fall on my knees before God after every uncaring verbal outburst, but still leave the grip of anger in my life untouched.

The life-change God longs for, and that we long for ourselves, comes by practicing the life of Christ to the point where it becomes habit and joining that effort to the supernatural work of the Holy Spirit in our lives.[23] The church of old, in its great wisdom, understood that the cardinal problem of human life was how to conform the soul to an absolute standard of holiness. The answer was not a technique to combat sin but the whole-hearted practice of virtue by the power of God.[24] To shy away from this journey cheapens God's grace. Or as the Puritans would say, it would be a union with half a Christ.[25]

Lie No. 5: We're Alone with Our Efforts, and It's Effort Alone

The final lie that prevents us from enjoying true transformation is this: Life-change is a matter of answering God's challenge to "buck up." This lie tells us we're alone with our efforts, and a life of holiness will come about through our efforts alone. If that's true, we're in trouble, because none of us has what it takes to pull off complete, all-encompassing life-change. The truth about our own efforts is this: Whenever we act alone, we're completely helpless. We're inadequate, powerless to bring about even a fraction of the life-change we desire.

Acknowledging our inadequacy is the secret to one of the most successful programs for life-change ever, Alcoholics Anonymous. AA has helped more people experience real change than just about any other program that has ever come down the pike. The secret is found in the first two steps of the twelve-step program: admitting that you're powerless over what you're facing, and acknowledging that only a Power greater than yourself can fix it.[26] You and I need something outside of ourselves and greater than ourselves to help us address what's wrong with us. This is not a sign of weakness, but an admission of reality.

I once heard a story about Muhammad Ali, the great boxer, who in his prime possessed a larger than normal measure of self-confidence. The story goes that he boarded a plane and found his seat. When the flight attendant came down the aisle, she told the champ to buckle his seat belt.

"Superman don't need no seat belt," Ali declared.

Without even pausing, the flight attendant responded, "Superman don't need no airplane either. Buckle up!"

We all have limitations, weaknesses, and areas of need. We are not today, nor will we ever be, Superman or Superwoman. We need God to do for us what we can't do for ourselves. This is what Jesus was teaching when he said, "only God's Spirit can change you into a child of God."[27]

True life-change is not about will power, commitment, or perseverance. Real life-change is about what can happen to a human life in partnership with the living God. Transformation takes place when our weakness meets His strength. And the Bible reminds us that the very same power that raised Jesus from the dead is available to transform our lives.

UNWRAPPING GOD

As a Christian, you have the Holy Spirit within you. His entrance into your life came instantly at the time of spiritual conversion. But that doesn't mean you're completely filled with the Holy Spirit. We're commanded in Scripture to "be filled with the Spirit," or more accurately from the Greek, "be being filled" or "keep on being filled."[28] But this is not like a glass being filled with water. We are not vessels into which God pours a certain amount of the Holy Spirit. Instead, being filled is a relational issue. The Holy Spirit is a Person, which makes "being filled" a matter of our relationship with Him. To be filled with the Holy Spirit means that we allow Him to occupy, guide, speak to, and control every area of our lives.

Think of it this way: You already have as much of the Holy Spirit as you are ever going to have—but how much of you does the Holy Spirit have? In teaching this to my seminary students, I often bring two glasses of water and two packets of Alka-Seltzer to class. Into one glass I place a packet, but with the wrap intact, symbolizing the presence of the Holy Spirit, but not the filling. Into the second glass, I place a packet that has been unsealed, allowing the Alka-Seltzer to fill the glass with its bubbles and fizz.

Turning to my students, I say, "Note something of enormous significance here. Both glasses have the Alka-Seltzer, just as all Christians have the Holy Spirit. But notice how you can have the Holy Spirit but not His filling." The goal of Christians is to live in such a way as to unwrap the packaging around the presence and power of the Holy Spirit in our lives.

C. S. Lewis reminds us that Christ says:

> Give me all. I don't want so much of your time and so much
> of your money and so much of your work: I want you. I have
> not come to torment your natural self, but to kill it. No half-
> measures are any good. I don't want to cut off a branch here
> and a branch there, I want to have the whole tree down. I
> don't want to drill the tooth, or crown it, or stop it, but to
> have it out. Hand over the whole natural self, all the desires
> which you think innocent as well as the ones you think
> wicked—the whole outfit. I will give you a new self instead. In
> fact, I will give you Myself: my own will shall become yours.[29]

So how do we unwrap God? There is only one way: We allow Him to have our whole selves by cooperating fully with His work in our lives.

British churchman John R. W. Stott reminds us that while sanctification—the process of becoming holy—is a *natural* consequence of our relationship with God, it is not an *automatic* consequence.[30] The Bible warns us not to "hold back the work of the Holy Spirit"[31] by deciding not to cooperate with what God wants to do in our lives. Sanctification as an event is declared; sanctification as a process is a joint enterprise that involves our choices. With every choice, writes Lewis, "you are turning the central part of you, the part of you that chooses, into something a little different from what it was before. And taking your life as a whole, with all your innumerable choices, all your life long you are slowly turning this central thing either into a heavenly creature or into a hellish creature."[32]

This is the goal of the journey before us—to bring desire, knowledge, and power together, traveling through what novelist Joseph Conrad called the "heart of darkness" in order to arrive at Augustine's "City of Light." This journey of sanctification, which arrives at its destination only when we make the journey with God and allow Him free rein in our lives, truly is a long night's journey into day.

Gaining Emotional Control

The Journey from Anger to Restraint

When something is in fashion, we say, "It's all the rage." But what do we say when the rage is rage itself?

A young father of four is pummeled to death at a youth hockey game. An enraged airline passenger wreaks havoc on a cross-country flight. Isolated incidents? Hardly. Leonard Ingram, founder of the Anger Institute of Chicago, contends that one out of every seven Americans is on the verge of exploding in an act of violence. And the statistics back him up.

Air rage incidents around the world increased four-fold from 1994 to 1997 alone. Road rage took the lives of more than two hundred people between 1992 and 1997 and left another 12,610 injured. Workplace violence, virtually unheard of until the 1970s, was costing businesses more than $36 billion a year by 1995. At the beginning of the twenty-first century,

Leon James, professor of psychology at the University of Hawaii, calls ours the "Age of Rage."[1]

Let's take a test. First, holding this book in your hand, stand up. That's right, stand where you are with book in hand. It's okay; you've looked stupid before. Now, I'm going to describe a situation. If you have ever lost your temper over the type of situation I describe below, you can sit down. I don't mean just mild irritation, I mean you *really* lost it. So there's some grace here.

Here's the first situation: If you got ticked off when I asked you to stand up, sit down.

Still standing? Okay. Next scenario.

You go to the grocery store. You're in a hurry. You get the two or three things you need, go to the line that says "Cash Only, Ten Items or Less," and the person in front of you has at least thirteen items. And writes a check.

If that has ever yanked your chain, sit down.

Since you may still be standing, looking kind of foolish, let's thin the ranks a bit.

You're on the interstate…

Sat down already? If not, let's go ahead and play it out. You're on the interstate, and you get stuck behind a car that's going fifty-five in a sixty-five-mile-per-hour zone. You can't pass, the driver ignores you when you ride his tail and flash your headlights, and to confirm his utter inability to navigate the roads, his left turn signal is still flashing from when he pulled onto the freeway from the ramp.

Seated yet? If not, here's one more: *in-laws.*

Gotcha.

Now, for those of you still standing, how long have you had this problem with lying?

VICTIMS OF ANGER

I don't know about you, but I'm amazed at how easy it is to give in to anger. One of my children can step out of line, make a mess, do something annoying—something really minor—and anger can immediately consume me. Or if I'm running late and get behind a slow car or catch a red light or two, my anger comes to the surface with alarming speed. My wife and I can have a perfect morning, and then one little thing is said or done, or not done, and where I was once ready to kiss her good-bye before I left, all I want to do is storm out the door.

Like so many of the deadly sins, anger is easily embraced—maybe the most easily. Perhaps it's because, as Frederick Buechner notes, anger is the most fun. "To lick your wounds, to smack your lips over grievances long past, to roll over your tongue the prospect of bitter confrontations still to come, to savor to the last toothsome morsel both the pain you are given and the pain you are giving back—in many ways it is a feast fit for a king." Yet Buechner is wise in carrying the meal through to its final course. "The chief drawback," he continues, "is that what you are wolfing down is your-self. The skeleton at the feast is you."[2] Think about what it would be like if you *weren't* consumed by anger. Consider the freedom of not having your RPMs instantly rush into the red zone, affecting you emotionally for hours, even days. Imagine what it would do to your relational world—in your marriage, with your kids, or with your colleagues at work. Think about all that you've done in anger that you'd give anything to take back. The unwise words. The hurtful deeds.

The Bible doesn't overstate our condition when it says an angry person does "foolish things."[3] Not many of us would argue that point. Just think what releasing your anger would do for you *physically*. The death rate for men who are quick to lose their temper is five times that of the average male, with the chance of a heart attack alone doubling.[4]

In light of the devastation caused by anger, it's no surprise that this is one of the most important areas to explore when you want to invite the power of God to transform your life. Unchecked and allowed to run its course, anger is perhaps the most destructive sin not only to ourselves, but also to those around us.

GIVING ANGER ITS PLACE

As destructive as anger can be, it stands alone among the deadliest sins in that it contains elements of righteousness. Pride is always evil. Greed is never anything but harmful. Sloth, lust, gluttony—they're uniformly damaging. Anger alone holds certain redeeming qualities that flow from the character of God.

Jesus is our model for how to harness the force of righteous anger. He once entered a synagogue on the Sabbath and encountered a man with a shriveled hand. The religious leaders at that time were threatened by Jesus' teachings and miracles, so they were intent on finding a way to discredit Him. Here was a perfect opportunity. They knew Jesus had this little habit of reaching out to hurting people, so they purposefully positioned a man within the synagogue who was in need of a healing touch. It was a violation of Jewish law to do any work on the Sabbath—even to heal someone. But hoping to trip Him up, the religious leaders were counting on Jesus' not being able to resist a chance to end the man's anguish. As soon as Jesus healed the man, the leaders could rush forward to accuse Him of acting improperly on a holy day. Caught in the middle was an innocent hurting man who was being used as a pawn in their sick little game. The religious leaders didn't look into his eyes and feel his pain, much less try to imagine what it must be like to go through life with a disabling condition. They simply needed him as bait.

Jesus encountered the man and had His own heart break. While He was feeling compassion for the man's suffering, He also saw into the hardness of the hearts of those who were using the broken man in such a callous manner. The next thing we see is the One who modeled the perfect, sinless life getting *angry*. Read the biblical record:

> When he went into the synagogue, there was a man there whose hand was shrivelled, and they were watching Jesus closely to see whether he would heal him on the Sabbath day, so that they might bring a charge against him. Jesus said to the man with the shrivelled hand,
>
> "Stand up and come out here in front!"
>
> Then he said to them,
>
> "Is it right to do good on the Sabbath day, or to do harm? Is it right to save life or to kill?"
>
> There was a dead silence. Then Jesus, deeply hurt as he sensed their inhumanity, looked round in anger at the faces surrounding him, and said to the man,
>
> "Stretch out your hand!"
>
> And he stretched it out, and the hand was restored."[5]

Anger is a human emotion that was given to us by God. It is often the most appropriate reaction we can have, providing the most holy and righteous response to the wrongs that we encounter. It can also provide the necessary fuel to act, driving us to do what most needs to be accomplished to set things right.

This was the case of a London pawnbroker who became a Christian and decided to enter full-time ministry. Traveling the country, he shared God's word with all who would listen. Somehow, though, the full-time vocation of teaching and preaching the Bible didn't seem to grip the former merchant as he thought it would. So he resigned from the ministry and returned to London.

One day as he was strolling through the East End slums, he noticed that every fifth building was a pub. Inside, men would loiter the entire day, drinking away their families' livelihood. Many of the pubs even provided steps at the counter so that small children could climb up and order gin. Outraged, this man once again began to preach, mostly outside the East End pubs. One day in 1865 a group of missionaries heard him speaking outside the Blind Beggar. They asked him to lead a series of meetings they were holding in a large tent. Though tormented and ridiculed by the locals, even enduring the injury of thrown stones, this man knew he'd found his destiny. It didn't matter that he had to suffer the bloody wounds from being pelted with stones. He was convinced that God had called him to bring the love of Christ to the slum dwellers of London's East End. Whenever he was tempted to give up, his passion was surely reignited by the image of the steps that enabled small children to order alcohol at the bars. Before long, the man founded a mission to care for those he was trying to reach. By the time he died in 1912, the mission was at work in fifty-eight countries. The man's name was William Booth, and the mission he started was the Salvation Army.[6]

If you never give righteous anger a place to take hold of you, you may never accomplish what God most wants done. Living your life the way God desires involves feeling what God feels, seeing what God sees, reacting the way God would react. Jesus entered the synagogue, saw a man suffering from a physical deformity, and responded with compassion. At the same time, His anger was ignited by the hardhearted religious leaders. As the early church father John Chrysostom wrote, "He who is not angry when he has cause to be, sins."[7]

UNRIGHTEOUS INDIGNATION

Anger has a righteous dimension that we need to harness, but that doesn't grant us an excuse to give it free rein in our lives. The Bible adds a needed caution: While not all anger is bad, it must always be controlled. The wisdom book of the Bible, Proverbs, reminds us, "A fool gives full vent to his anger, but a wise man keeps himself under control."[8] A fool lets his anger take over, giving it full expression with no attempt at restraint. A wise person knows the necessity of self-control, which reminds us that anger is not something that directs us, but something that we need to direct. This life lesson goes well beyond anger, in fact, and applies to all of life.

I once read how Frederick the Great of Prussia was walking on the outskirts of Berlin when he encountered a very old man proceeding in the opposite direction. Approaching the man, Frederick asked, "Who are you?"

"I am a king," replied the old man.

Frederick laughed and said, "A king! Over what kingdom do you reign?"

"Over myself," the old man replied.[9]

The realm of the self is the one kingdom that God calls us to rule, and exercising self-control is the one way to keep that kingdom from being destroyed. When a powerful emotion such as anger is not controlled, no matter what you are angry about, it can escalate into a destructive force that is nothing less than nightmarish.

I read about a road rage incident in Philadelphia. A driver cut in front of another motorist on the expressway, and the affronted motorist killed the driver who had the gall to cut in line. Traffic had slowed as it was funneled into a single lane. The murderer claimed that he had waited in line for more than a quarter of an hour until he could begin to enter the flow of traffic. Just as he was about to do so, another car passed him on the shoulder of the highway and cut in line. And as though that weren't enough, the offending driver laughed and made an obscene gesture at him.

The angry motorist took a gun from his glove compartment, walked up to the other man's car, and shot him to death.[10] Anger can turn into a bludgeon that leaves a trail of bodies—figuratively and literally—in its wake. So the simple wisdom given to the apostle Paul by the Holy Spirit rings clear: "In your anger do not sin."[11]

A CULTURE OF ANGER

We live in what linguistics professor Deborah Tannen calls "the argument culture," which drives us to indiscriminately approach the world—and the people in it—in an adversarial role. This culture rests on the assumption that opposition is the best way to get things done.[12]

Consider the judge who issued a restraining order between two people because they couldn't seem to get along. The interpersonal conflict had even become violent, quickly growing to involve members of both parties' families. The incident that led to the court action occurred on the playground at Boston's Charles River Park. The antagonist's name was Jonathan, and the young woman who had action brought on her behalf was named Stacy. Nothing particularly unusual about this scenario, except that these two parties were both three years old.

The parents of one three-year-old went to a judge to make the other three-year-old "play nice." Apparently Jonathan made Stacy cry and tried to kick her. So her mother filed an assault and battery complaint against the little boy. A superior court judge issued a restraining order that dictated that the mothers must keep their children supervised and separated while at the playground. Violators would be held in contempt, fined, or even jailed. One of the lawyers involved admitted that the whole thing was ludicrous. But notice what the mother who brought the action said about the other mother: "This was the only way you could send this woman a message."[13]

THREE TRUTHS ABOUT ANGER

Most of our attempts to keep anger under control fail because of faulty assumptions and unrealistic expectations. We falsely believe that anger is our right, that it's the best response, and that in certain circumstances it's beyond our control. This approach has led to everything from parents badgering Little League umpires to acts of international terrorism. There has to be a better way, and not surprisingly, we find it in the Bible.

Most of the ways we mishandle anger can be traced back to three myths we believe about life. First, that things should go our way, no matter what that means for the rest of the human population. Second, that anger comes from external causes. And third, that our anger is beyond our control. Let's look at these myths in detail and also examine the biblical truth that supplies the solution to anger.

The Truth: Things Won't Always Go Our Way

Because we are born with a fallen nature, it comes naturally to us to look out for our own interests first, above all else. This leads to our belief in the myth that the world and everyone in it should be dedicated to doing what is in *our* best interest. The myth leads to our assumption that the actions of others and the circumstances we find ourselves in should all work together to our benefit. This is a lie that fuels a lot of unrighteous anger.

The Bible exposes the lie in plain words. According to Jesus, "In this world you will have trouble."[14] Even if we've been exposed to this truth, we still don't want to believe it. This denial of reality is similar to our reaction to the knowledge that earthly life ends in death: We all know we're going to die; we just don't believe it will ever happen to us. Likewise, we know that things won't *always* go our way, but we're still shocked when the tables are turned and reality comes crashing down.

A high school student made a list of what it would take for his day to qualify as a good one: "I need to wake up to my favorite song playing on the radio at the exact time my clock radio goes off. I have to wear my favorite jeans, shirt, and shoes. My breakfast cannot include oatmeal, scrambled eggs, or bran. I have to get the front seat on the bus. And all of my friends need to say nice things to me all day long."[15] I don't think this kid has ever had a good day. Or ever will.

Here's a reality check:

When you go to a movie, there will be times that a guy who was the starting center on his college basketball team will sit in front of you.

You'll go to a restaurant, and the service will be slow, and the food will be cold.

You'll get stuck in traffic when you're running late.

Your spouse won't always say what you want him to—or listen when you need her to.

The grocery store checkout line will stretch back to the frozen foods section while five wonderfully motivated employees who *could* open another line stand off to the side so they can compare shades of lip gloss.

In this world, we'll have trouble. It was true in Jesus' time, and it's still true today. We live in the real world, while our anger feeds off a fantasy world where everything always goes our way. To get on top of anger we have to recognize the truth captured in a paraphrase of a popular bumper-sticker slogan: "Stuff happens." Accepting that will help you stay a bit calmer when the stuff starts coming your way.

The Truth: No One Else Causes Our Anger

Once we accept that the world isn't devoted to our personal comfort and convenience, we have a second myth to confront: the lie that says our anger is caused by external circumstances. The truth is that no one *makes* us angry; our anger comes from inside us. Our emotions are internal, so it does no good to try to blame anyone else. It's time to stop saying, "*You* make me so mad I can't see straight! I was fine until *you* made me act this way."

As long as we blame others, we feel justified in our outbursts. After all, we're simply victims of circumstance who react with the response that's clearly called for. This is a lie that needs to be banned from our thinking.

The truth is clear: Our anger arises from within. It tells us that something is going on, but it's going on *inside us.* Even righteous anger flows from deep within, triggered by the Holy Spirit, but accepted or rejected by our own spirits. Anger is never merely outside of ourselves—it is our internal reaction.

The anger that wells up inside us may be a reflection of hurt or feelings of rejection. It could be a sign of fear or a sense of helplessness. It could flow out of raw fatigue. Yet an angry reaction to life is just that, a reaction. The thing that prompts the reaction is outside of us, but the expression and extent of our anger comes from inside. It's not someone else's fault when I lose my temper. It's mine alone.

"Anger is intensely personal," observes William Ezell. "It is the quintessential individual signature emotion. I am what makes me mad."[16] This is not merely a human insight. Jesus challenged us to look deep within when He said, "Your true being brims over into true words and deeds."[17]

Our feelings and emotions often are transformed into expressions of anger. This is perhaps most clearly seen with children. When they don't get their own way, they throw a tantrum. They yell, scream, kick, and cry. Because of their lack of maturity, they give themselves over to what has happened. We can't imagine an airline traveler, going to his gate only to find out that the flight has been cancelled, throwing himself to the ground in the middle of the terminal, kicking and screaming, "It's not fair! It's not fair!"

Or can we? Think how often you've seen a business traveler whose flight is delayed or canceled stomp his foot, throw down his briefcase, utter a few words of profanity, and then spend fifteen minutes reading the riot act to an innocent airline employee behind the counter, announcing to the world that he'll never fly that airline again.

A mature person is able to look at a small child and see the tantrum as an indication of what's inside the child, a reaction that is grossly out of proportion to the situation at hand. We need to apply the same objective distance and perspective to ourselves. "Anger," noted Seneca, "will cease and become more controllable if it finds that it must appear before a judge."[18] The Bible calls us to preside over that court. We are the judge who issues the necessary restraining order, something the Bible calls self-control.

The Truth: We Control Our Reactions

Just as it's a lie that anger comes from external circumstances, it's also untrue that anger is a force beyond our control. We're the ones who choose to control our anger, or choose to let it rage. The Bible expresses a truth that affords us the greatest experience of God's power—the experience of exercising control. The writer of Ecclesiastes tells us, "Do not be eager in your heart to be angry."[19] And in James, the Bible says, "be...slow to become angry."[20]

To be eager, or slow, is a purposeful response, a choice that God puts fully within our control. These are decisions of the will that are superimposed over our circumstances and emotions. This is not about submerging or denying our feelings, but ruling our spirit. It's about taking the time to consider what's going on and then bringing ourselves under control. This is easy to say, but how does it work when we're seeing red?

THE JOURNEY FROM ANGER TO RESTRAINT

God commands us to take control of our anger, so how can we plug into His power to enable us to obey this command? It starts with exercising the discipline to tell ourselves the truth.

Taking control of our anger is a practical matter that relies on a few tools that are readily at hand. Psychologist Albert Ellis developed a strategy called the ABC approach, which establishes a framework for effective anger management.[21] First, let "A" represent a particular event that happens to you. Then let "B" represent what you say to yourself about that event. What you say to yourself can be right or wrong, good or bad, helpful or harmful. Then let "C" represent your emotional reaction to what you have said to yourself about what happened to you.

Let's go back to the grocery store. You're standing in the ten-item express checkout line. A woman in front of you is taking *forever*, and you're in a hurry. She has at least twenty items—double the limit. She chats with the checkout clerk, she ignores her kids while they run wild, and then she *writes a check* instead of paying with cash.

That's A, the circumstance you find yourself in.

Immediately, you start talking to yourself. That's B, what you tell yourself about this event. It's a conversation you probably aren't even aware of.

Soon you react to what you've told yourself. That's C. Let's go ahead and look at C.

If you're like me, you've told yourself that this woman is way out of line, and your reaction is one of being put upon. You start off with a simple glare to let everybody know how you feel. If that doesn't register, you let out a hard sigh. Then you cross your arms. You repeatedly, and somewhat dramatically, glance at your watch. Then it's time for another sigh. (There really is an art to this.) Finally, you innocently ask, loudly and with feeling, "Excuse me, isn't this the *EXPRESS* checkout lane for *TEN* items and *CASH ONLY?*"

In other words, you act like you're five years old.

Now let's play with this scenario. The lady ahead of you in the checkout line, whom we're calling A, didn't cause your incredibly immature reaction, which we're calling C. Your reaction actually was caused by B, the message you sent to yourself about what happened. You concluded that this woman was insensitive, self-centered, and bent on holding you up.

That interpretation of the circumstances led to your anger, and by repeating the message you gave full expression to your anger. The woman didn't make you angry; *you* did.

Let's go back and look at what I said to myself—consciously or not—that made me get upset. First, I told myself that things have to go my way for me to be happy. That meant that the line had to speed up or I'd be unhappy.

Second, I told myself that people should be perfect. The woman in front of me should have had ten and *only* ten items. Her children should have behaved impeccably. She should have paid in cash. And she should have completed her transaction in less than three minutes. But this woman had the nerve to be imperfect, and I told myself that imperfect behavior was unacceptable.

Finally, I told myself that the whole thing was somebody else's fault and that my anger was the fault of the customer who was taking so long. But that was a lie. My anger came from myself—more specifically, from my reaction to what the woman did.

Almost every scenario where my temper is aroused can be thought of in these terms. Whenever I encounter a situation that doesn't go my way, I can feel aggrieved and explode in anger, or I can tell myself the truth about what's going on. Or more accurately, I can choose to *listen* to the truth—for the Holy Spirit is working within me to prompt me away from inappropriate and sinful anger. All too often, I simply choose to ignore His still, small voice that speaks calming truth to me about the circumstances of my life. But when I stop and listen, the insight is there. It's the free offer of the power of God operating in my life. As I cooperate with what God wants to do in and through me, that power is unleashed to overcome my anger.

This is the challenge behind the Bible's reminder that "a man's discretion makes him slow to anger."[22] Discretion refers to our reflection, our choices, our assessment of things, and when utilized, it joins with God to help cultivate a slowness to anger in spite of circumstances.

A CHILD SHALL LEAD US

In 1960, white parents in New Orleans openly opposed a federal court decision that ended segregation in the city's public schools. Not only did white parents withdraw their children from any school that admitted blacks, they picketed the schools that did.

One child, six-year-old Ruby Bridges, was the sole African-American student at her school, which meant that for a long period she was the only student of any race attending that school. For weeks she had to be escorted by federal marshals as she walked through a gauntlet of angry citizens who unleashed malicious verbal assaults—assaults that sought not only to wound this little girl, but to incite anger in her heart.

The bait was never taken, though. Ruby Bridges approached her school, and the crowds, without anger. Instead, a calm, serene spirit blanketed her every step.

One day, her teacher saw her mouthing words as she passed the lines of angry, abusive white parents. When the teacher reported this to child psychiatrist Robert Coles, who was working in a New Orleans hospital, he became curious. What had the little girl said?

When asked, Ruby said she'd been praying for the parents of her white classmates. Coles was perplexed. "But why?"

"Because they need praying for," she answered. She had heard in church about Jesus' dying words, "Father, forgive them, for they know not what they do." This was the Spirit's deeper truth being spoken to a human heart.

This little girl decided to take God's truth to heart.[23] We can do likewise, if we choose. God's power gives us the power to take responsibility for our anger, to stop blaming others, and to exercise control over our reactions to life's circumstances. Like Ruby Bridges, we can take this truth to heart and experience the dramatic life-change that results when we draw on God's power to enable us to exercise restraint and let go of anger.

A Matter of Resolve

The Journey from Sloth to Diligence

If you've ever been in a Christian bookstore or card shop, you've probably seen a plaque or bookmark, print or wall-hanging, featuring a story called "Footprints in the Sand." It tells of a man who dreamed that he saw his life in terms of a walk along the beach with God. Throughout the years, there were two sets of footprints. One was his, and the other was God's. Yet he noticed that during the most difficult times of his life, only one set of footprints appeared in the sand. In his dream, he asks God about the single set of footprints and is told that those were the times God carried him.

"Awww."

Let me give you a new and improved version that a friend e-mailed me.

> One night I had a wondrous dream,
> One set of footprints there was seen,
> The footprints of my precious Lord,
> But mine were not along the shore.

But then some stranger prints appeared,
And I asked the Lord, "What have we here?
Those prints are large and round and neat.
But Lord, they are too big for feet."

"My child," he said in somber tones,
"For miles I carried you alone.
I challenged you to walk in faith,
But you refused and made me wait."

"You disobeyed, you would not grow,
The walk of faith, you would not know.
So I got tired, I got fed up.
And there I dropped you on your butt."

Because in life, there comes a time,
When one must fight, and one must climb,
When one must rise and take a stand,
Or leave their butt prints in the sand.

For some reason, I don't think I'll see that one hanging from a wall, much less printed on a greeting card. But it probably should be, because it speaks to one of the most critical barriers to the transforming work of God in our lives, the sin of sloth. We don't hear about sloth much these days, but it's a good word, one we ought to get reacquainted with, because it holds a major key to life-change through the power of God.

As described by Dorothy Sayers, sloth is that "which believes in nothing, cares for nothing, seeks to know nothing, interferes with nothing, enjoys nothing, loves nothing, hates nothing, finds purpose in nothing, lives for nothing, and remains alive only because there is nothing it would die for."[1] Or in a one-word assertion that many in our day put forward, sloth merely says, "Whatever." Yet as all-encompassing as these descriptions might be, sloth is specific in its manifestations.

THE SIX FACES OF SLOTH

When families visit the zoo, no one beats down the door to the sloth cage. Not a particularly handsome animal, the sloth is a slow, lumbering beast that bears no special marks and boasts no vivid colors. Each one looks very much like the next, and none of them are much to gaze at. Yet the sin that carries the same name wears many disguises and is easily missed as it takes on various forms. Consider the following six faces of the sin of sloth.

Laziness

The first, and most visible, face of sloth is laziness. The Bible says of some people that they're so lazy "they won't lift a finger to feed themselves."[2] This is the image most of us have of sloth—*extreme* laziness—and we're all susceptible to it. Our culture has programmed us to expect a life of ease. It's not just that we wish everything were easy—we think everything *should* come to us in abundance with no effort on our part.

If life's circumstances are inconvenient or don't suit us for any reason whatsoever, we feel justified in giving up. If I have to work at it or if it's going to take a long time, then something's just not right. We see no fault in ourselves; the fault lies squarely with the difficult or elusive goal that we sought to achieve. If it turns out to require too much effort, then it's just not worth doing. We decide what to pursue based on the ease of achieving it.

The danger in these assumptions is great. Some of the best things in life demand effort and are worth every moment of the toil. The best marriages have been worked on, regularly, for years. The best businesses have been labored over. Even our spiritual growth is reflective of our faithful investment. G. K. Chesterton once quipped, "The Christian ideal has not been tried and found wanting. It has been found difficult, and left untried."[3] It's no wonder that God, through the prophet Jeremiah, asked "who is he who will devote himself to be close to me?"[4]

We don't want to hear that following God involves sacrifice, effort, work. Left to myself, I want a version of cheap grace that makes salvation and the obedient life easy. I want a spiritual life, but I don't want it to involve hard work, and certainly not sacrifice. I would prefer my personal soul work and the influence it has on the world to be achieved as in the movie *Pay It Forward.* In that story, on the first day of school a teacher writes the following assignment on the chalkboard: "Think of an idea to change the world—and put it into action!" Intrigued, a boy named Trevor dedicates himself to a simple plan: Do three good deeds, and then ask each recipient to do three good deeds for someone else. Soon, peace and love and goodwill will cover the world. It's a movie, so of course the modest investment of six or seven hours' worth of work alters the trajectory of the entire planet.

Essayist Mark Oppenheimer notes that such trivial understandings of what is truly involved in personal life-change, much less global change, can be found in everything from *Chicken Soup for the Soul* books to "What

Would Jesus Do?" bracelets to the amazing intervention of angels in the lives of characters on television dramas. All promise a good outcome, but without making any real demands on anyone. "Just Do It" does not, after all, mean "Just do this 100 miles a week of cross-country running that marathoners do"; it means "Just buy the shoes—swift feet sure to follow."[5] Essayist and social critic Henry Fairlie suggests that sloth could be described as the hatred of all things spiritual that require effort, or faint-heartedness in matters of difficulty in striving for perfection.[6] Or as Chaucer's Parson reflects, "it will endure no hardship nor any penance."[7] Sloth is diametrically opposed to Christ's great challenge to pick up our cross and follow. Jesus assumes decisive action; sloth seeks inaction.

Tolerance

Sloth goes beyond laziness to influence many other areas of life, including how we regard other people. Tolerance has become a cultural buzzword. We are told to accept any behavior by any person, regardless of how that behavior might conflict with our beliefs and convictions. But when sloth gets mixed up with tolerance, it guides how we regard not just others but *ourselves*. Sloth leads us to tolerate who we are, and to accept how we are, so that we turn a blind eye to personal deficiencies that we really need to examine.

In recent years, we've seen an enormous emphasis on getting in touch with ourselves by learning our personality types and temperaments, following our spiritual giftings, and being loyal to our passions. This is helpful when it guides us in becoming more effective in carrying out God's plan according to the unique design he has given each one of us. The dark side, however, is using how we are "wired up" as an excuse for not attending to the person we need to *become.* Quite frankly, as sinful humans, being true to who we are is not always the best course of action. The sin of sloth can lead us to ignore the problems in our lives and the areas that we need to change, to the point of resigned, unconcerned acceptance of sin. Sloth skims over those areas with a shrug of the shoulders and a dismissive "Well, what can you do?" When sloth takes hold, there's nothing we *can* do. Or perhaps more accurately, there's nothing we *will* do.

Apathy

Sloth produces laziness, and it tolerates personal sins that should be dealt with. But it doesn't stop there. Sloth often appears in our lives in the form of apathy. Philosopher Søren Kierkegaard declared, "Let others complain that the age is wicked; my complaint is that it is wretched, for it lacks passion."[8] Whereas tolerance leads us to accept personal failings that should be addressed, apathy leads us to desensitize ourselves to issues in our lives that we should be passionate about.

Apathy isn't simply a neutral indifference; it actually holds the potential to do real harm to others. One of the most tragic events of the last century occurred in New York City. A young woman from Queens named Kitty Genovese was stabbed to death after being chased by an assailant for thirty minutes and attacked three times in the street. During this vicious crime, thirty-eight neighbors watched from their windows without coming to the young woman's aid. Not a single person offered help or ran into the street to disrupt the crime. They didn't even bother to pick up the phone and call the police.[9]

It's not an isolated instance.

In May of 2000, a thirty-year-old mother of six died in Miami. She had been brutally attacked. Stabbed and bleeding, she staggered from door to door, pleading for help. Despite her obvious injuries and her desperate pleas, no doors were opened, no help was offered, no phone was lifted. She collapsed dead in a driveway.[10]

The sin of sloth breeds a kind of moral numbness. We see, but we don't feel, much less care. Our hearts are moved by film portrayals of courageous revolutionaries, such as Scottish freedom fighter William Wallace in *Braveheart* or activist Erin Brockovich, but we often let the feelings of the movie cheaply satiate the parts of us that would rise to the challenge of being more than merely hearers of the word.[11]

It is in this sense that Vaclav Havel, the last president of Czechoslovakia and the first president of the Czech Republic, and one of Europe's foremost playwrights and essayists, would write to his wife, "It is not the authors of absurd plays or pessimistic poems, nor the suicides, nor people constantly afflicted by anger, boredom, anxiety, and despair, nor the alcoholics and drug addicts, who have, in the deepest sense, lost their grip on the meaning of life and become 'nonbelievers': it is people who are apathetic."[12]

Procrastination

A fourth destructive face of sloth is its persuasive whisper that there is no need to hurry, we'll get around to it another time. Sloth robs us of a proper sense of urgency.

Procrastination is knowing what we need to do, but never quite bringing ourselves to do it. We keep putting off until tomorrow what is not absolutely required to be done today. But reasons for further delay proliferate, so what cries out to be done seems to never fall under the "required to be done today" banner. Then the inexorable progress of time consumes the last opportunity we had to act, an opportunity now lost forever.

Human life is built on seizing the hour given to us, and whether the moment is grasped often becomes all-determining.[13] As the wisdom of the book of Proverbs reminds us, "A farmer too lazy to plow his fields at the right time will have nothing to harvest."[14]

Our society's movement away from farming the land to working in factories has dulled us to a proper sense of urgency. Technology has given us such recourse for our failure to act that procrastination is allowed to take root and develop for years before its note comes due. Not so for those in ancient times who were tied to the land. Sloth's procrastinating nature was readily seen, and appropriately feared, as reflected in the morality tales of the day. The most legendary, told by Aesop, finds a group of ants busy one winter's day drying their store of corn, which had become damp during a long spell of rain. Up came a grasshopper who begged them to spare a few grains. "For," she said, "I'm simply starving." The ants stopped work for a moment, though this was against their principles. "May we ask," they said, "what you were doing with yourself all last summer? Why didn't you collect a store of food for the winter?"

"The fact is," replied the grasshopper, "I was so busy singing that I hadn't the time."

"If you spent the summer singing," replied the industrious ants, "you can't do better than spend the winter dancing." They laughed, and then went back to work.[15]

We may feel insulated today from the consequences of procrastination, but even the protection of technology can be stripped away. In 1999, the term Y2K entered our vocabulary. The embedded chips and microcontrollers that had become the guardians of our lives suddenly had the potential to derail the very life they allowed us to live. It was all going to happen on January 1, 2000, and it had to be fixed.

Computer programs that supported the day-in, day-out systems that served our lives used only two digits instead of four to indicate the year when designating a date, so 1999 was just 99. On January 1, 2000, unless the computer code was reviewed and repaired, many computers would assume that we were entering the "new" year of 1900, which could cause widespread computer failure.

Suddenly our advanced technology had brought us to a real sense of urgency. We had to get our nation's computer systems "Y2K compliant," and quickly. This was worth the incredible financial cost to pay programmers to review the computer code that ran operating systems for everyone from local, state, and federal government to Fortune 500 corporations to the local grocery store. The big problem wasn't money; it was time.

Computer code had to be painstakingly checked line by line. And there were millions of lines of code to review and repair. The Social Security Administration started working on its Y2K problems in 1991. Four hundred full-time programmers were assigned to the project. By mid-1996, after five years of steady work, they had only reviewed and repaired six million lines—just 20 percent of the total. A company like AT&T had *five hundred million* lines of code. The U.S. Defense Department had as many as one billion.

Then there was the challenge of getting to embedded chip systems, not to mention those on satellites, on the ocean floor, and inside buried pipelines. Adding to the challenge was that there were as many as five hundred different software languages in use, and many of them were no longer understood by younger programmers. And even if everything got repaired, it still needed to be fully tested.

Nobody knew what would happen if the code wasn't changed. It could have been a small bump in the road that caused some minor inconveniences in select areas—which proved to be true—or it could have been absolutely catastrophic. Nobody would know until it came, but the possibilities were frightening. Social Security checks could stop coming; commercial jetliners all over the world could be grounded; credit card charges could be rejected; military defense systems could fail; police records and emergency communications could be inaccessible; there could be massive, long-term power failures; telephone systems could shut down; traffic signals could stop functioning; and business after business could fail, leading to massive unemployment and economic depression.

The problem had been known about for years. But it was always someone else's issue, someone else's concern. The only reason we ended up meeting the Y2K challenge was because we *had* to. January 1, 2000, became the greatest nonnegotiable deadline in history. But so is tomorrow.

Activity

We've seen that sloth mitigates against initiative and productivity. Yet a fifth face of sloth, ironically, is activity itself. We can fill our lives with busy-ness, events, and recreation to the point that we never attend to the matters that most need our attention. Or as Eugene Peterson notes, busy people are too lazy to take control of things.[16]

Robert MacNeil, for years the front half of PBS's *MacNeil-Lehrer News Hour*, once wrote that by the age of twenty, the average person has watched at least twenty thousand hours of television. As we age, we can add about ten thousand hours per decade so that we've watched forty thousand hours of television by the age of forty. The only thing we do more than watch television is sleep. MacNeil then encouraged his readers to think about what they could do with even a fraction of that time. It has been estimated that you can earn a college degree with about five thousand hours worth of effort. In ten thousand hours, you could learn enough to become an astronomer or an engineer, learn several languages fluently, or walk around the world and write about it. The biggest problem with something like television is what we *didn't* do with that time.

But missed opportunities are only part of the story. Underneath such missed investments is an emptiness of heart, an emptiness of life, an emptiness of mind, and an emptiness of soul, because we're not attending to what we need to attend to.[17] MacNeil ends his essay by observing, "Almost anything interesting and rewarding in life requires some constructive, consistently applied effort. The dullest, the least gifted of us can achieve things that seem miraculous to those who never concentrate on anything."[18]

The mandate of modern existence is to fill our time with activity, even empty, meaningless activity. Such activity joins hands with the deadly sin of sloth by preventing us from investing ourselves in what matters. We succumb to whatever activity presents itself rather than answering the challenge of investing our efforts in what is truly important. We retire at the end of the day, having raced through our crowded calendars, quietly congratulating ourselves on our self-importance. In truth, it is sloth stroking our egos while blinding us to the futility of all our busy-ness.

Circumstance

The final face of sloth is the assumed importance of life's circumstances. It's easy to exaggerate the power of circumstances, allowing the situations we encounter to dictate our lives. Certainly there are things that come down the pike that can't help but affect us, seasons of life and situations of living that shape the contours of our existence. Yet there are numerous times when the things that come our way don't warrant capitulation, but instead require bold action to overcome the obstacle. Sloth tells us not to bother, to just give in to the situation. Sloth ascribes power to the circumstance, not to the person.

Solomon saw it differently. "The lazy man is full of excuses. 'I can't go to work!' he says. 'If I go outside I might meet a lion in the street and be killed!' "[19] There are many "mights" in life and even more obstacles that pose genuine problems. Yet sloth would have us surrender to our circumstances, to allow the situation to define us rather than our taking charge and redefining the situation by rising above it.

A daughter once complained to her father about how difficult things had become for her. "As soon as I solve one problem," she said, "another one comes up. I'm tired of struggling."

Her father took her to the kitchen, where he filled three pots with water, placing each on a hot burner. Soon the pots came to a boil. In one he placed carrots, in the second, eggs, and in the last, ground coffee beans. He let them sit and boil, without saying a word.

The daughter waited, wondering what he was doing. After a while, he turned off the burners. He fished out the carrots and placed them in a bowl. He pulled the eggs out and placed them in a bowl. Finally he poured the coffee into a bowl.

Turning to her he asked, "Darling, what do you see?"

"Carrots, eggs, and coffee," she replied.

He brought her closer and asked her to feel the carrots. She did and noted that they were soft. He then asked her to take an egg and break it. After pulling off the shell, she observed the hard-boiled contents. Finally, he asked her to sip the coffee. She tasted its rich flavor.

"What does it mean, Father?"

He explained that each of them had faced the same adversity—boiling water—but each reacted differently. The carrot went in strong, hard, and unrelenting, but after being subjected to the boiling water, it softened and became weak. The egg was fragile to begin with. It went into the water with nothing more than a thin outer shell protecting its liquid interior. But after enduring the boiling water, it was hardened almost beyond recognition.

The ground coffee beans were unique, however. By being in the boiling water, they changed the water.

The father asked his daughter, "Which one will you be?"[20]

THE JOURNEY FROM SLOTH TO DILIGENCE

As we have seen, sloth can not only render us ineffective in life, but it can also do real damage to those around us. Sloth is so subtle, however, that it can disguise itself as everything from harmless inactivity to intense and seemingly meaningful activity. It can dart quickly underneath any excuse. It can hide its face behind apathy. It can rob us of the desire we need to achieve true life transformation. Until the challenge of sloth is answered, the knowledge and power God would bring to change our lives is kept at bay. Yet the Bible offers a three-fold path that exposes sloth in our lives and leads us to rise above it.

Step One: Realize the Truth
Victory over sloth begins with the realization that creating the life we long for involves *doing something,* instead of taking the easy route of doing nothing. The Bible tells us that "lazy men are soon poor; hard workers get rich.... Lazy people want much but get little, while the diligent are prospering."[21] Sloth tells you just the opposite. It argues that laziness, tolerance, apathy, procrastination, meaningless activity, and inviting every

little circumstance to sideline you are the optimum ways to live. It's the path of least resistance that will feel the best, taste the best, and deliver the most.

We must realize that's not true.

Let's say you want to lose weight. Somebody offers you a donut. You think to yourself, *I'm on a diet, so I have to say no.* But you don't *want* to say no, because everything inside of you equates saying no with unhappiness. Happiness, you believe, is found in eating the donut. This makes dieting very hard and not very successful. When you make the donut the optimum life investment, you're operating on a skewed value system. The truth, of course, is that you're not saying no to the taste of a donut, you're saying yes to the kind of body you want. You're saying yes to a higher level of health. Suddenly what was negative has become the positive thing that you seek.

The late Tom Landry, legendary coach of the Dallas Cowboys, once quipped that his job as a coach was to get a group of men to do what they didn't want to do so they could achieve the one thing they had wanted all their lives. In the business world, this is called *alignment*. When a business aligns itself, it realizes that it must take the organization's core values and purposes and translate them into the day-in, day-out activities of the organization. From goals to strategies, policies to procedures, budgets to hiring, the *purpose* of the company must be directly translated into the *practice* of the company. It is alignment, perhaps above any other quality, that marks the truly exceptional companies.[22]

But alignment is not beneficial only to an NFL team or a successful business venture. It marks the life of an individual who has wrenched himself free of sloth. A sloth-free life aligns its actions with what it wants to achieve. As the author of Hebrews would counsel, "Let us strip off anything that slows us down or holds us back…and let us run with patience the particular race that God has set before us."[23]

Step Two: Resolve to Act

The second step in defeating sloth is to make a personal resolution to take action. The path of sloth, choosing *not* to do something, is an act of the will. The antidote to sloth, the resolve to take effective action, is also an act of the will. The issue is raw desire. But desire that is never acted on dies.

There are millions of people who would like to write a book, yet few authors ever see their words in print. In the preface to his first novel, *A Time to Kill,* John Grisham writes that he made up his mind that he wouldn't be a person who just talked about writing a book; he was going to be one who did it. He committed to writing one page a day until the book was finished. No matter what came up, he'd write one page a day.

Now he's one of the best-selling novelists of our time. His resolve mattered. It matters to any life.

Consider the industry and output that flowed from the life of Thomas Jefferson. Author of the Declaration of Independence, broker of the Louisiana Purchase, sponsor of the Lewis and Clark expedition, lawyer, scientist, philosopher, musician, architect, businessman—Jefferson was the epitome of a Renaissance man. In a letter to his daughter, he revealed his secret: "It is wonderful how much may be done if we are always doing."[24]

Yet resolve runs far deeper than the commitment to be disciplined in the use of one's time. It's a question of wholesale devotion. This is the idea behind the Bible's admonition in Ecclesiastes: "Whatever your hand finds to do, do it with all your might."[25] It is said of the stirring performance of top athletes that they "left everything on the field." The life of resolve leaves everything on the field of life. Such resolve will eclipse all other factors and serve to release your full potential.

I once read of a group of seasoned climbers who were going to make an attempt on Mt. Everest. Before they left the United States to make their assault on the legendary peak, each was questioned at length by a psychiatrist. The doctor asked each of them, "Will you get to the top of Everest?" Some said, "Well, I'm going to do my best" or "I'm sure going to try" or "I'm going to work at it."

However, one of the climbers, a slightly built man who seemed the least physically impressive, had a decisively different reply. When the psychiatrist asked him the question, he thought for a moment, and then answered, "Yes, I will."

He was the first one who made it to the summit.[26]

Step Three: Refuse to Stop

The third ingredient in the antidote to sloth is the refusal to give up. There has to be persistence, a dogged determination to remain faithful to the end. In 1 Corinthians, the apostle Paul writes that we should "stand firm." He then adds, "Let nothing move you. Always give yourselves fully to the work of the Lord, because you know that your labor in the Lord is not in vain."[27] In the midst of a diligent, devoted life, we'll be tempted to throw in the towel, to take ourselves out of the game. To resist that temptation, we must purpose to do something in our heart, and then refuse to be sidelined no matter what comes along. Sloth will tempt us at our weakest and most vulnerable moments of fatigue and discouragement. To refuse to stop, to refuse to quit no matter what, is the only way to finish the race that is set before us.

In October 1998, Lynn Brooks competed in her *nineteenth* Hawaiian

Open Ironman Triathlon, a grueling competition that involves a swim in the open ocean of more than two miles, followed by more than one hundred miles of biking, and ending with a full marathon run. Featured in an NBC-TV program on the event, Brooks recalled that one year, during the marathon leg of the competition, she left the race and entered an aid tent. With her body aching and her emotions drained, the desire to stop was overpowering. In the tent, sitting on a bench, was a man drinking an ice-cold beer. Reading the athlete's thoughts, he said, "All you have to do is drop out of the race like me."

Suddenly, Brooks said that she realized his words were the message of the devil. She left the aid tent and re-entered the race. Reflecting on the moment filled her eyes with tears. "It was the hardest, and most *glorious,* day of my life."[28]

HUMAN RESOLVE PLUS DIVINE POWER

Americans failed to embrace the 2000 Olympics in Sydney with the same passion and interest as previous Olympic contests. NBC marked some of the lowest ratings ever for an Olympic telecast. Whether it was because of the time difference, the way it was covered, or because it was later than normal in the sports year—with baseball ending and football beginning—we simply didn't enter into its pathos.

Yet one scene broke through and gripped the nation. American Laura Wilkinson came from behind to win the gold medal in the ten-meter platform dive. Several months prior to the games she had broken her right foot in three places—an injury that continued to cause extreme pain. The fact that she competed despite the broken bones made her victory a stunning achievement. After winning the championship, when Wilkinson was asked by a reporter to put into words the emotion she was feeling, she quoted her favorite Bible verse: "I can do all things through Christ who strengthens me."[29]

Christians understood the meaning behind the words. As Wilkinson gave of herself, God met her on the diving platform, giving her strength and encouragement in spite of her physical pain. Wilkinson's personal resolve, joined to God's power operating within her, resulted in an astounding achievement.

But the reporter interviewing the diver didn't quite know how to respond. This wasn't the usual "I'd like to thank God and my mother" answer one normally expects from an athlete. Collecting her thoughts, the reporter shifted gears and attempted to change the subject: "How much beyond your expectations was this?"

"At first," Laura responded, "I thought it was impossible. But I just wanted to go out there and dive for God, for everybody, for everybody who ever dreamed."[30]

WHAT GOD CARES ABOUT

I have a theory. Though it's only a hunch, I think if I had time, I could make a strong case from the Bible for its basic contours. My theory is that when this life is over and we stand before God to give an account for our lives, what we were most worried about won't be at the top of His agenda. We're going to be focused on all that we've done that we *shouldn't* have done —those youthful indiscretions on prom night, those questionable deductions taken on last year's tax return—and that's okay. All of those things matter. But I think God may be more concerned about all that we *haven't* done, all that we refused to try, and all that we never cared about. This is why sloth is a deadly sin, for it's primarily a sin of omission. It is a sin of neglecting what's right.[31]

Much of what you'd like to change about your life right now looms large—so large, in fact, that changing it seems impossible. Sloth will rear its head and try to get you to hold that thought. Sloth wants you to give up, stop trying, and stop caring. Sloth desperately wants you to let your desire for life transformation die.

But there's another way. You can let yourself dream and then take that dream and start diving. For you're not diving alone; God is diving with you. And you can do all things through Christ who will strengthen you.

Gods of the Stomach

The Journey from Gluttony to Moderation

The earliest set of table manners that we know of date from the thirteenth century and reveal a clear sense of decorum. When it came to food, gnawing a bone and putting it back in the dish was verboten. Falling upon the dish like a swine while eating, snorting disgustingly, and smacking the lips was not recommended. The Emily Posts of that era also counseled against spitting over, or on, the table, and urged restraint when it came to blowing your nose into the tablecloth.

How about putting back on your plate a morsel that had previously been in your mouth? Not plan A. And speaking of things that had been in one's mouth, people were encouraged to refrain from coughing or blowing their nose in such a manner that might project something onto the table. Probably a good call.[1]

Today, while manners still count, we've had to add a few more rules to the game of eating. We've had to do this not because table decorum is slipping, but because we're fat. Eating has taken such prominence in our culture that "[the] Golden Arches are now more widely recognized than the Christian cross."[2] We revere eating so much that we've been forced to invest in programs like Dr. Atkins's diet "revolution" or bottles of Metabolife to stimulate our fat-burning capabilities. Prescription drugs like Meridia are taken to try to regulate the brain's appetite-control center.[3]

If you're a guy and want a rippled midsection before you hit the beach, then you can write out a check to the Pierre Company. They'll provide you with a spray-on abs kit, complete with stencils, a small bottle of tinting solution, and a sixteen-ounce can of pressurized polyurethane. Low-priced packages guarantee that your new abs will stay on for about eight hours, long enough for a good day at the beach. Higher-priced kits, for those longer vacations, promise a full twenty-four hours of the buff look.[4]

Too much hassle? Try the Fat-Be-Gone ring that promises to trim hips, buttocks, and thighs just by slipping it onto a finger. Or give Aoquili Defat Seaweed Soap a chance to wash the fat right down the drain.[5]

Some people tire of the endless procession of weight-loss schemes and decide to simply glory in their larger-than-average size. The National Association to Advance Fat Acceptance (NAAFA) was founded in 1969 and now boasts more than fifty local chapters. Beyond the laudable goal of ending discrimination based on body size, they attempt to help members accept their weight and reject the idea that less might be more. Indeed, NAAFA's goal is to create and sustain a "fat subculture" in America.[6]

Still, the pills and diets, and the acceptance or rejection of being overweight, all fail to address the core problem: the gluttony that fuels our appetites. As a deadly sin, gluttony is the most visible, yet it's seldom taken seriously. It's considered less a sin and more a harmless lapse of moderation. Nan Lyons, a novelist and frequent contributor to *Bon Appetit*, writes that gluttony "may be viewed as a harmless overindulgence, to be cured not by soul-searching but by the occasional dose of Pepcid AC."[7] Or as C. S. Lewis's fictitious senior devil, Screwtape, informed the younger demon Wormwood, "one of the great achievements of the last hundred years has been to deaden the human conscience on [this] subject, so that by now you will hardly find a sermon preached or a conscience troubled about it."[8]

Yet the apostle Paul made it clear that any overindulgence that affects our health always matters, because what we do with our bodies affects our spiritual health. This is more readily understood in sexual matters than in terms of our stomachs, yet the very fall from Eden came about as a result of disobeying God in terms of eating, and the second Adam—Jesus—was tempted along similar lines.[9] What is arguably the greatest and most theologically significant of the sacraments—the Lord's Supper—was ordained to involve a meal. There was something about consumption, something tied to our stomachs, that needed to be engaged. Gluttony was not placed on the ancient listing of the deadliest of sins without deep reflection and keen observation of human realities. Perhaps it would help us gain a mastery over this sin if we were to look carefully at its true appearance, particularly its two most common faces.

THE FACE OF OVERINDULGENCE

The first face of gluttony is the most obvious: overindulgence. In 2000, a report was released from the Worldwatch Institute that found for the first time in history that there were as many people in the world who were overweight—1.1 billion—as there were people in the world who were underfed.[10] And if there is an obesity capital of the world, it's America. At the beginning of the twenty-first century, 61 percent of the population in the

United States was overweight—up from 56 percent in the early 1990s, with 27 percent of all adults considered medically obese.[11]

Of course, we all know this is a problem because every day, around 65 million Americans are dieting. The sales of diet books outrank all other books on the market except for one—the Bible.[12] We've even made liposuction the most popular form of cosmetic surgery. A study in 1995 found that at mid-decade, more than a hundred tons of fat were being removed from American bodies through surgery every year. By 1999, there were four hundred thousand liposuction procedures in the United States alone.[13]

Few characters in literature have captured the essence of the face of gluttony more colorfully than Augustus Gloop in Roald Dahl's *Charlie and the Chocolate Factory*. Augustus was "so enormously fat he looked as though he had been blown up with a powerful pump. Great flabby folds of fat bulged out from every part of his body, and his face was like a monstrous ball of dough with two small greedy curranty eyes peering out upon the world."[14]

Willy Wonka had announced that five golden tickets would be hidden in five chocolate bars and that the lucky finders would be granted a tour of his mysterious and wonderful chocolate factory. Augustus was among the first of the finders. The poor, underfed hero of the tale, Charlie, along with his parents and four grandparents, read the news.

> "I just *knew* Augustus would find a Golden Ticket," his
> mother had told the newspapermen. "He eats so *many* candy
> bars a day that it was almost *impossible* for him *not* to find
> one. Eating is his hobby, you know. That's *all* he's interested
> in. But still, that's better than being a *hooligan* and shooting
> off *zip guns* and things like that in his spare time, isn't it? And

what I always say is, he wouldn't go on eating like he does unless he *needed* nourishment, would he? It's all *vitamins,* anyway...."

"What a revolting woman," said Grandma Josephine.

"And what a repulsive boy," said Grandma Georgina.[15]

The grandparents were right. Yet eating to the point of excess is nothing new. In ancient Rome, beautifully tiled, but understandably sparsely furnished, vomitoria were built into the finest homes for the express purpose of allowing the residents to eat all they could hold, go and vomit, then return to the table to continue to gratify their appetite. Servants were even trained in the practice of "throat-tickling" to help guests at major fetes keep the rhythm of eating and vomiting in sync. Nero was once able to use this approach to engage in a thirty-six hour banquet. Even the famed Seneca joined in, declaring, *"vomunt et edunt, edunt et vomunt."* Vomit and eat, eat and vomit.[16]

The more you weighed during Tudor times, the larger your fortune was perceived to be. Further, substantial girth was equated with heroic valor and was a sign that a man was to be taken seriously. His body was meant to be an extension of his weaponry.

As anyone can tell from the most casual glances at his portraits, Henry VIII was obviously determined to be a formidable ruler. At a typical dinner, Henry could be relied upon to consume an entire joint of lamb and to reduce a small deer to a pile of bones. He would then move on to a pair of lobsters and several plovers, followed by a calf's head pie. The meal would then be topped off by a dessert of gingerbread and quince tartlets. By 1547, at the age of fifty-six, Henry had to be carried from room to room because of his immense size. At the time of his death, his distended stomach could no longer be contained by his clothing, and the circumference of his chest measured nearly sixty inches. The irony is that Henry VIII's favorite dish was the humble artichoke, which has almost no calories.[17]

Indulging in such gluttonous excess leads to enormous consequences. First, we get overweight. Physically, this creates countless health problems and drastically shortens our life span; emotionally, it can destroy our self-esteem. But overeating is only one expression of gluttony. Consider, as well, the overindulgence of alcohol, which is rampant. It leads to spouse abuse, child abuse, traffic fatalities, loss of jobs, and the destruction of health. While alcoholism is often referred to as a "disease," we must be careful to avoid speaking too glibly of it as a sickness.

While there may be physical and even psychological conditions that make some more likely than others to be susceptible to abusing or becoming addicted to alcohol or drugs, by far the greater part of gluttony within our lives is willful. Psychiatrist Gerald May has concluded that the symptoms of addictive personality are caused more by the addiction than a pre-existent condition. We have addict*ed* personalities, as opposed to addict*ive* personalities.[18] The seemingly innocent, tame, benign face of gluttony is an appetite without restraint, which can not only cripple a life, but wars against the very image of God, for what marks an animal is that it knows only its appetite. When our appetites become our defining mark, the image of God is deeply marred.

THE FACE OF OVEREMPHASIS

Overindulgence is but one dynamic of gluttony—there is also the overemphasis it breeds in regard to our bodies. It is difficult not to make our physical appearance the ultimate barometer of our sense of self-worth and accomplishment, embracing our culture's glorification of the size-two supermodel as the one and only acceptable reflection in the mirror.

Model Magali Amadei, featured in such international fashion magazines as *Vogue, Elle,* and *Cosmopolitan,* calls the images of women appearing in such magazines "very unrealistic." She says that photos of her are retouched to make her breasts appear larger, her waist thinner, and her legs longer. The focus on her body, coupled with her own tendency toward perfectionism, led to a habit of bingeing and purging. She was finally pushed to seek help following an incident in which she took thirty laxatives and ended up on the bathroom floor during a photo shoot. When she told her agent that she wanted to go public with the fact that she was a recovering bulimic, her agent cringed. "Eating disorders are not a pretty picture," notes the model, "and the fashion industry is all about a pretty picture."[19]

This face of gluttony can result either in being overweight or underweight. In either case, it's a matter of obsessing over what we put in our mouths. Many refrain from eating or drinking in excess, but fixate on counting calories, adding up fat grams, measuring carbs, getting on the scales every day, measuring portions, poring over diet and nutrition books, and analyzing every angle of their bodies in the mirror. Anorexia nervosa, the pathological fear of weight gain leading to extreme weight loss, has become nearly epidemic on college campuses, affecting 5 to 7 percent of America's twelve million undergraduates. It carries a death rate of 20 percent —the highest of any mental disorder.[20]

In his book *Telling Secrets,* Frederick Buechner helps us see that this overemphasis is more than merely cosmetic:

> One of our daughters began to stop eating. There was nothing
> scary about it at first. It was just the sort of thing any girl who

thought she'd be prettier if she lost a few pounds might do—
nothing for breakfast, maybe a carrot or a Diet Coke for
lunch, for supper perhaps a little salad with low calorie dress-
ing. But then, as months went by, it did become scary.
Anorexia nervosa is the name of the sickness she was suffering
from, needless to say, and the best understanding of it that I
have been able to arrive at goes something like this. Young
people crave to be free and independent. They crave also to be
taken care of and safe. The dark magic of anorexia is that it
satisfies both of these cravings at once. By not eating, you take
your stand against the world that is telling you what to do and
who to be. And by not eating you also make your body so
much smaller, lighter, weaker that in effect it becomes a child's
body again and the world flocks to your rescue. This double
victory is so great that apparently not even self-destruction
seems too high a price to pay.[21]

THE LESS-THAN-GRAND ILLUSION

Like most sins, gluttony offers an illusion we are only too ready to
embrace—perhaps the greatest sleight of hand attempted by any of the
deadly sins. We take the desire that exists within us for life as it was meant
to be, and for life in relation with God, and instead of orienting our life
toward that, we turn to cheap substitutes and pale imitations. As John
Eldredge has observed about so many areas of life, we mistake the water
hole for the sea.[22] We try to address our deepest desires with a momentary
escape, a quick hit, a fast charge. We eat too much, or drink too much, or
obsess over eating and drinking too much, all the while attempting to

quench the thirst of our soul. Not only are we left thirsty, but we're now vulnerable to greater self-destruction.

C. S. Lewis observed that in such ways, gluttony can act as a kind of "artillery preparation" for other attacks. "Keep him wondering what pride or lack of faith has delivered him into your hands," his fictional demon Screwtape counseled, "when a simple inquiry into what he has been eating or drinking for the last twenty-four hours would show him whence your ammunition comes."[23]

Gluttony was once thought to eclipse even pride as the root of all sin. Indeed, it was seen as the *source* of pride. In premodern and classical times, both the quality and presentation of food marked one's place in society. There was glory in the display and the expense. It was also the means of rank, for where one sat to dine reflected one's standing and social prominence.

This feature remains today. While studying at Oxford, I was invited to dine at "high table" one evening at Christ Church College. The ancient dining hall features a single long table at the head of the room, elevated on a dais, perpendicular to the long rows of tables arranged before it. There is no attempt to soften the difference between those at high table and those seated at tables on the crowded floor. We alone were asked to be in coat and tie; we alone were served wine; we alone were waited on individually. The class distinction was obvious and intentional. That was the honor of "high table."

But gluttony does much more than appeal to our hunger for status or social rank. At its heart, this sin redirects our appetites from God's desires to the desires of the flesh. Too much food deadens our spiritual senses, which is why fasting has long been prescribed for heightened spiritual awareness. Too much drink puts us at the mercy of our basest instincts. From this, one seventeenth-century sermonizer referred to gluttony as lust's "forechamber."[24] As the prophet Habakkuk declared, it is through gluttony that we are often betrayed.[25]

THE JOURNEY FROM GLUTTONY TO MODERATION

How can we move past the excesses of gluttony and live our lives not just in moderation, but in fullness? How can we become sensitized and energized by God, as opposed to being dulled and deadened by the misuse of food and drink? The Bible would point us toward a strategic set of considerations.

Recognize the Temple You Live In

First, we must see our body for what it is in relation to God. Most of us have no concept of what our body really is, even though the Bible tells us: "Do you not know that your body is a temple of the Holy Spirit, who is in you, whom you have received from God?… Therefore honor God with your body."[26] Our body is a sacred place where God dwells through His Holy Spirit. When it comes to flesh and blood, we're on holy ground.

Most of us have a sense of the sacred. If someone were to take a Bible and rip it to shreds in front of you, it would be a bit disturbing. If you were to enter into a church's sanctuary and find that someone had defiled it with profane graffiti, it would be a violation beyond the typical scrawl on a subway wall. Why? Because when you hold a Bible, or enter a church, there is a sense of the transcendent, the sacred, the "other"—that there really is such a thing as holy ground.

The truth is that church architecture does not reflect the image of God. And though the words are inspired by God, the paper and leather of a Bible are not indwelt by God. Not so with your body. There you are dealing with something that God not only made, but, if you are a Christ-follower, actually inhabits. Your body is not just flesh and blood. A spiritual dynamic is inextricably intertwined with your body. Deepening your awareness of this breeds moderation in your appetite, for gluttony—whether it's being overweight, abusing your body through drugs or chemicals, or smoking cigarettes—wars against the presence of God. This connection is highlighted in the New Testament in relation to wine, where being drunk with wine and being filled with the Holy Spirit are juxtaposed, but the idea carries forward throughout all of the dimensions of life that gluttony can invade.[27] Gluttony cheapens your life and deadens the core of your being. If you fail to honor and protect your body, the neglect can't help but diminish the filling and work of the Holy Spirit.

As such, gluttony should elicit disgust, which William Ian Miller contends is gluttony's only true remedy[28]—either disgust at ourselves or the disgust of others toward us. The opposite of disgust is attraction—attraction to what a God-honoring body represents. Intriguingly, this seems to be the sentiment of Scripture, such as when the apostle Paul counsels us to "offer your bodies as living sacrifices, holy and pleasing to God—this is your spiritual act of worship."[29]

Determine Your Identity

Second, you have to know yourself for who you are. You're not simply what can be seen in the mirror, yet it is this reflection that often leads to our drift toward excess. Who you are goes much, much deeper. Many are in need of this simple truth.

A young girl named Martha attended a large public school near Indianapolis. Being shy, she didn't have very many friends. She had the unfortunate distinction of reaching her senior year in high school without ever having a date. During the fall of her senior year, a popular girl named Julie was assigned as her lab partner in chemistry. Julie invited Martha to a Halloween party, Martha's first invitation to a party in ten years.

Understandably nervous, she walked through the door of Julie's home, tried to say hello to the few people she knew, drank a soft drink, and stood on the edges of the groups of people, listening in on conversations.

In one corner stood a group of boys. They would look around the room, talk in low voices, and then burst out laughing. Suddenly, Martha realized they were all looking at her. Then they laughed louder than ever. She didn't know what to do but turn away and try to hide.

Later in the evening, a boy she hardly knew sat down near her, and she remembered that he'd been part of the group that was laughing. Gathering up her courage, she asked him what had elicited their laughter. He told her they'd been playing a game in which you look at people and try to determine what animal they look like. He told her that Julie, the popular girl, was easy—she was a deer. Mark was a giraffe. Cheryl was like a chipmunk.

"What about me?" Martha nervously ventured. "You did me. I saw you."

"Sure," he said. "You were a dog." Then he started laughing all over again.

When Martha went home and looked in the mirror, that's what she saw. A dog. For years, whenever a boy would look at her, that's what she felt in her heart that he saw. And whenever she looked at herself, the words came to her over and over, "You're a dog. You're a dog."[30]

What's running through your heart and mind when it comes to who you think you are? Is it a superficial sense of beauty? Is it a defeating echo of words that binds you to a sense of failure and insecurity, making your physical appearance everything to you? Countless numbers of people operate from a perceived deficit or, at the opposite end of the spectrum, cling to a sense of worldly beauty as their source of identity. As a result, they've never been able to go any further with who they really are. They hate the way they look, so they eat. Or they are so obsessed with being thin that no matter how much they lose, it's never enough.

Here's the truth. When we look in the mirror, the thing that matters the least in terms of personal value and self-worth is the reflection. It certainly matters the least to those around you. Haven't you ever met a beautiful woman, or a handsome man, and your first impression is very strong because of how the person looks? But then, after only a few minutes with them, because of who they are and the way they act, their physical appearance has not only lost its luster, but can actually be repulsive? The opposite is also true, isn't it? We've all met people who, at first, may not have appeared particularly attractive. Then, within minutes, we see a beauty that is beyond description. The longer we know them, the more attractive they become. Scripture speaks to this. In 1 Peter, the apostle writes, "Don't be concerned about the outward beauty that depends on fancy hairstyles, expensive jewelry, or beautiful clothes. You should be known for the beauty that comes from within, the unfading beauty of a gentle and quiet spirit, which is so precious to God."[31]

So what *does* matter when you look in the mirror? What *should* your self-image be based on? The foundation is what God sees when *He* looks at you. And if you will allow a synthesis of a great deal of Scripture, paraphrasing it for simplicity, here are His words:

I willed you into existence. Everything about you was done by careful design. And I only made one of you; there will never be another. So make no mistake about who you are. You are My precious child. Your identity and worth will always rest in Me. If you want to grow in beauty, then come to Me. Enter into a relationship with Me. Come to Me for the forgiveness of the ugliness of sin, and I will make you as beautiful and pure as winter's first snow.

One who understood this was the Skin Horse in the classic children's book *The Velveteen Rabbit,* the tale of a stuffed toy rabbit, all clean and new, who becomes "real." During that process, the Rabbit meets an old, worn-out, but very much loved, stuffed horse. Their dialogue has much to teach on the subject of what matters most in terms of who we are:

> The Skin Horse had lived longer in the nursery than any of the others. He was so old that his brown coat was bald in patches and showed the seams underneath, and most of the hairs in his tail had been pulled out to string bead necklaces. He was wise, for he had seen a long succession of mechanical toys arrive to boast and swagger, and by-and-by break their mainsprings and pass away, and he knew that they were only toys, and would never turn into anything else. For nursery magic is very strange and wonderful, and only those play-things that are old and wise and experienced like the Skin Horse understand all about it.
>
> "What is REAL?" asked the Rabbit one day, when they were lying side by side near the nursery fender, before Nana came to tidy the room. "Does it mean having things that buzz inside you and a stick-out handle?"

"Real isn't how you are made," said the Skin Horse. "It's a thing that happens to you. When a child loves you for a long, long time, not just to play with, but REALLY loves you, then you become Real."

"Does it hurt?" asked the Rabbit.

"Sometimes," said the Skin Horse, for he was always truthful. "When you are Real you don't mind being hurt."

"Does it happen all at once, like being wound up," he asked, "or bit by bit?"

"It doesn't happen all at once," said the Skin Horse. "You become. It takes a long time. That's why it doesn't often happen to people who break easily, or have sharp edges, or who have to be carefully kept. Generally, by the time you are Real, most of your hair has been loved off, and your eyes drop out and you get loose in the joints and very shabby. But these things don't matter at all, because once you are Real you can't be ugly, except to people who don't understand."[32]

Find What Satisfies Your Soul

The first two steps are essential. But God doesn't stop there. He goes on to give us a third challenge: Fill your soul with that which satisfies. The virtue of moderation that defeats the sin of gluttony will come only when we cease to look toward our excesses for fulfillment.

When Satan tempted Jesus in the wilderness, one of the temptations revolved around food. Jesus was hungry, and Satan came up to Him and said, "If you are the Son of God, tell these stones to become bread."[33] This wasn't just a reference to satisfying physical hunger; it presented the temptation to satisfy His deepest needs through instant gratification and to make the pursuit of catering to His stomach the purpose of His power and strength, devotion and divinity. Notice how Jesus responded: "It is written, 'Man does not live on bread alone, but on every word that comes from the mouth of God.' "[34]

An intriguing answer.

Jesus tells Satan that our deepest desires can indeed be filled, but not through bread alone. If we make it bread alone, we will never truly live.

Jesus attempted to teach the same truth to His disciples when they urged Him to eat, worried that He wasn't consuming enough. " 'I have food to eat that you know nothing about.' Then his disciples said to each other, 'Could someone have brought him food?' 'My food,' said Jesus, 'is to do the will of him who sent me and to finish his work.' "[35]

Our lives must draw strength and sustenance, pleasure and enjoyment, satisfaction and meaning from more than what we eat, feel, taste, drink, or shape through diet and exercise. Bread alone will never give us what we long for. We need to eat from the table of God and find satisfaction in Him. C. S. Lewis, in his essay "The Weight of Glory," notes that we must give in to *stronger* desires. "We are half-hearted creatures, fooling around with drink and sex and ambition, when infinite joy is offered us," he reflects, "like an ignorant child who wants to go on making mud pies in a slum because he cannot imagine what is meant by the offer of a holiday by the sea."

"We are," he concludes, "far too easily pleased."[36]

Only God truly satisfies our soul. Only God can provide the soul-deep pleasure that we seek. The lie of gluttony is that pleasure is enjoyed best when we satiate the physical urges of the stomach. But the truth is just the opposite. Exercising moderation in the things of this life, eating and drinking included, frees us to enjoy the One who satisfies our deepest hunger. Only orienting our life toward God will secure that which we hunger for in our deepest parts.

Knowing Who You Are

The Journey from Envy to Security

The Academy Award–winning film *Amadeus* is one of the most thought-provoking movies you'll ever see. It takes its title from the middle name of the famous composer Wolfgang Amadeus Mozart. Choosing Mozart's middle name as the film's title was purposeful, for Amadeus means "beloved of God." The movie explores our feelings about how God bestows His grace, a dynamic that plagues the main character of the film, who, intriguingly, is not Mozart but a man named Salieri, a contemporary of Mozart and a composer of lesser talent.

The conflict begins in 1781, when Mozart is invited to play for the emperor's court, where Salieri serves as the court composer. Mozart's genius is unmistakable. When he finishes his performance, everyone in attendance is astounded. It is then that Salieri realizes that the musical gift he has sought from God for so long has been given to another.

And there could be little doubt of Mozart's gifting. He first composed a minuet and trio for the keyboard when he was six years old. By the time he was twelve, he was writing constantly, creating in the course of his career seventeen operas, forty-one symphonies, twenty-seven piano concertos, dozens of piano sonatas, along with music for organ, clarinet, and countless other instruments. It was said that he could actually imagine one piece as he wrote down another, and that he could see an entire composition in his head before he committed it to paper.

To Salieri, this musical genius proved that Mozart was the one beloved of God, while Salieri himself seemed to have been overlooked by God. That was hard enough, but Mozart's character in the film is filled with arrogance, temperamental fits, drunkenness, sexual immorality, and irreverence. Unlike Salieri, Mozart had never asked God for the gift. And the great composer never seemed grateful for it. In the end, it is this that drives Salieri not only to madness, but to murder.

The opening scene of the movie reveals the aged, guilt-ridden Salieri cutting his throat and then being taken to an asylum. Sometime later, a priest visits to try to reach out to this lost soul. In Salieri's confession to the priest, we learn that when it became apparent that God wasn't going to bestow him with a degree of talent or fame in league with that given to Mozart, his heart hardened. Taking a crucifix, he declares to God, "From now on, we are enemies." The crucifix is then thrown into the fireplace.

In the end, giving in to a single emotion led Salieri to kill everything he held dear. He ends up hating God, hating Mozart, and hating himself.[1] The all-destructive emotion that overwhelmed his life? The deadly sin of envy, which Herman Melville aptly called "the rabies of the heart."[2]

THE DESTRUCTIVE POWER OF INSECURITY

None of us is completely immune to envy, since its roots start forming very early in life. From childhood on we are compared to others, observes psychologist Solomon Schimmel. Our value as individuals often is measured by how much dumber or smarter, weaker or stronger, poorer or richer we are in relation to our peers.[3] This comparison creates a singular condition that is often confused with envy's lesser cousin, jealousy. The heart of jealousy is a sense of rivalry with another, flowing from a fear of loss—loss of stature, loss of relationship, or loss of achievement. Envy is far more lethal, however, because it extends the damage in our lives far beyond jealousy's petty concerns. Envy seeks to destroy us by unleashing a three-fold pestilence, beginning with cut-loose desire, which leads to dislike, and then ultimately to destruction.

The Pestilence of Desire

Envy has its genesis when we see something desirable that belongs to another person. It could be physical appearance, a job, money, talent, position, a spouse, even children. The other person possesses something that we want. Envy is a vice of proximity—the closer someone is to us in terms of vocation, temperament, gifts, or position, the more fertile is the soil in which envy grows. In the classic pattern, notes Cornelius Plantinga, the prosperous envier resents the rich, the 3:58 miler resents the 3:54 miler, the pretty resent the beautiful, and the hardworking B+ student resents the straight-A student, especially the happy-go-lucky one who never seems to study.[4] In his fictitious portrayal of hell, Dante drew from this aspect of envy and doomed the envious to having their eyes eternally sewn shut. All their lives they had allowed their vision to focus on others. Now their eyes were forever closed in punishment.[5]

The damage of envy doesn't end with the harm it does to *us*, however. The desire to have what others have extends to us wanting to stir the sin of envy in others. In fact, envy stands alone in this regard. There is nothing within us wanting to generate more pride and anger, more sloth or greed, within the heart of another person toward ourselves. Yet we have a natural predisposition to want to bring forth the sin of envy in others. And this isn't just a casual desire. Striving to become the focus of another's envy has few equals in terms of motivation and satisfaction. Knowing that others desire what we have breeds a sense of self-worth and security that props up our wobbling egos. That's the false reward of envy.

The Pestilence of Dislike

Envy never stops at wanting what another person has or striving to get someone else to want what we have. It goes on to breed dislike, even hatred, toward the one who possesses what we desire. This is captured in the word itself, which is drawn from the Latin *invidia,* which means "to look maliciously upon." The Greek term, as used in the New Testament, literally refers to having an "evil eye."[6] Envy keeps us from being able to admire that which is nobler or lovelier or greater than ourselves. Envy demands that we turn hostile toward that which is exceptional.[7] We don't like to talk about such feelings, preferring to disguise them as something else. Will Campbell recalls being told by one of his childhood mentors, "You know, Wee Willie, I don't hate anybody. 'Cause the Bible says it's a sin to hate. But there are some folks I hope dies of cancer of the tonsils."[8]

Envy can't help but bring such sentiments to the surface. When someone has something we don't have, or accomplishes something we haven't, envy can't celebrate. Instead, it grows resentful, taking the entire affair as a personal affront. This is what the Greek philosopher Aristotle saw when he reflected on the deadly nature of this sin, noting that people who succumb to its grip think that the person they envy is somehow getting what rightly belongs to *them*. They feel pain not simply because they desire something, but because the other person has what they desire. Aristotle notes that the envier is sick of a strange disease—that of another's health.[9] The Bible's enjoinder to "Rejoice with those who rejoice"[10] is the one thing that envy can't bring itself to do.

Envy begins by innocently asking, "Why shouldn't I enjoy what others enjoy?" but ends by demanding, "Why should others enjoy what I may not?"[11] The celebration of others comes across as a personal violation to the one who gives in to envy's power.

Even the soul that has previously stood strong against petty desires and dislikes can fall victim to the cutting edge of envy's blade. Irish writer Oscar Wilde once told a fictional tale about how the devil was crossing the Libyan desert. He came upon a spot where a small number of demons were tormenting a holy hermit. The sainted man easily shook off their evil suggestions. The devil watched as his lieutenants failed to sway the hermit, then he stepped forward to give them a lesson.

"What you do is too crude," he said. "Permit me for one moment."

He then whispered to the holy man, "Your brother has just been made Bishop of Alexandria." Suddenly, a look of malignant envy clouded the once-serene face of the hermit. Then the devil turned to his imps and said, "That is the sort of thing which I should recommend."[12]

The Pestilence of Destruction

Desire and dislike fail to fully describe envy's snare, because the deadly nature of this sin is not fully exposed without its third dimension: destruction.

When you give in to envy, you not only desire what another person has and resent him for having it, but you want to destroy its presence in the other person's life. What an envier ultimately wants is not simply what another has; what an envier wants is for another *not to have it.*[13] Frederick Buechner describes it as the consuming desire to have everybody else remain as unsuccessful as you are.[14]

Most of the time this is subtle. For example, Chuck Swindoll says we can take the "but" approach.[15] We say,

"He's an excellent salesman, but he isn't very sincere."

"Yeah, she's smart, but she doesn't have any common sense."

"She's a good surgeon, but she doesn't mind charging you for it."

The "but" approach is utilized when we reluctantly acknowledge a particular gift in someone, but then let envy quickly enter to destroy the other person's gift.

Then there's the "reversal" approach. Someone does a good job, and we cast a shadow over it by questioning the person's motive. We throw in a doubt, aspersion, or suspicion in an attempt to devalue the person's well-meaning gesture or laudable accomplishment. Somebody makes a generous gift, and we say, "Well, he's just trying to impress the rest of us." Another gets a promotion, and we snidely add, "Well, I wonder how *she* got the job."

Equally employed is the "unfavorable comparison." Someone does something noteworthy, and we respond by comparing the deed to someone else who did it better. John sings a solo, and the envy in us says, "Well, you ought to hear *Bill* do that one." You drive past a well-manicured lawn and say, "If you think *they* have a nice yard, you ought to see the one on the corner!" When we find that we can't do, experience, or enjoy the things that *others* can, we take our revenge by denying that those things had worth in the first place. Ironically, we try to negate the value of the things we envy, when we envied those things solely because they appeared to have more value than what we ourselves have.

The goals of the "but," "reversal," and "unfavorable comparison" approaches all remain the same: destruction of that which is envied.

The subtle nature of envy's destructive bent is not always verbal, much less even active. There is a silent version of envy's destructive tendencies. Consider the secret satisfaction we experience at the misfortune of others. The business leader who is relieved of responsibility, the politician who is disgraced, the priest caught in adultery. The Germans have a word for it, *schadenfreude,* which means finding joy in the suffering of another. Hence an envious conservatory student may feel privately delighted at the memory lapse of a rival during her recital performance. The pastor of a small church may act sad but secretly be elated that a more admired minister has been arrested for drunk driving.[16]

When such secret pleasure doesn't present itself through the natural course of events, or through the subtle subversion of the tongue, envy is more than willing to take a more direct approach. In a provocative French medieval romance, St. Martin is portrayed as coming upon two men, one greedy and the other envious. Being a saint, he instantly detects their shortcomings. He makes an offer, seemingly to address their respective vices: The one who asks for something shall receive it, but the other shall receive twice as much.

The greedy man doesn't answer first, hoping to be the beneficiary of the other man's wish. Yet the envious man pauses as well—he "dared not to ask according to his desire, for reason that he feared to die of grief and malice that his comrade's portion should be larger than his." Finally, threatened with a whipping by the greedy man, he lights upon a satisfactory solution. He asks St. Martin to remove one of his eyes, ensuring that while he might be visually impaired, the other man would be entirely blind.[17]

The wish of the envious man was harsh, but left unchecked, envy seldom stops even at this level of evil. In the famed case of Cain and Abel, where Cain's offering to God was less esteemed than that of his brother's, only murder itself would satisfy Cain's wounded ego.[18] This is why the Bible warns us of the sin of envy in such strong language: "If you harbor bitter envy and selfish ambition in your hearts, do not boast about it or deny the truth. Such 'wisdom' does not come down from heaven but is earthly, unspiritual, of the devil. For where you have envy and selfish ambition, there you find disorder and every evil practice."[19]

It's not difficult to see how distasteful envy is and how easily it earns its place on the list of deadliest sins. British writer Angus Wilson notes that envy "has the ugliness of a trapped rat that has gnawed its own foot in its effort to escape."[20]

We've seen the evil that envy produces, but what of its counterpart virtue? What did the church fathers identify as the virtue that cancels out envy and leads to lasting life-change?

THE JOURNEY FROM ENVY TO SECURITY

The solution to envy begins with recognizing why this sin possesses the power to prevent us from being transformed into the likeness of Christ. As long as we allow envy to set us on a course of desire, dislike, and destruction, we'll never be free to develop the life God calls us to. Envy, by keeping our focus on others, prevents us from investing in our own life-change.

Envy Keeps You from Developing Yourself

When you envy, you are focusing on others, which keeps you from developing *yourself*. I once read a quip that if the grass always looks greener on the other side of the fence, it's probably because you're not properly caring for the grass on your own side.[21] When all you do is look at others in envy, focusing on what they have—compared to what you don't have—you never do what it takes to become what God wants *you* to be. And it is in becoming who God made you to be that the security you long for becomes reality. The energy that is spent being concerned about what others possess could have been invested in creating your own place in the world and making your own mark on history. Envy carries a bitter irony—it draws your attention to what others have and then uses that preoccupation to ensure that you'll never have it.

There's a story from ancient Greece about a prized athlete who was so accomplished in the public games that his fellow citizens erected a statue in his honor. A rival, consumed with envy, went out each night to try to push the statue off its pedestal. Because of the size of this monument, the rival made very slow progress. One night, however, he was successful. As he finally tipped the statue off its pedestal, it fell back and crushed him to death.[22] This is the futility of envy—it lures all of our energy into the act of tearing down another person's accomplishments with the promise that somehow it will lift us up. Instead, it crushes the very promise of our life under its weight. Or, as in Aesop's fable of the caterpillar and the snake, the preoccupation with trying to become what another is destroys the unique nature of who we are.

Aesop imagines the caterpillar envying the colossal length of a snake. "Wishing to match length with the snake, he dropped down beside him and tried to stretch himself until he strained so hard that, before he knew it, he burst."[23] By envying the nature of the snake, the caterpillar destroyed his own nature. And envy has the same effect in our lives. In fact, it destroys the very life within us by preventing us from allowing the person we are in God to come to fruition. Yet God intends for every one of us to serve an infinitely important role in His kingdom. He created you and gifted you expressly for that purpose. Real life-change begins when you turn from envy and use that energy to pursue the unique and special life God has designed for you alone.

Envy Keeps You from Learning from Others

There's a second reason why conquering envy is critical to lasting life-change. If you give in to its wiles, it keeps you from benefiting from the wisdom and mentoring of others. Let's say someone has achieved a particular position that you'd like to achieve. Envy desires it, which soon gives way to resentment, and if left unchecked, eventually seeks to undermine the person and her achievement. All of which does nothing toward helping you achieve your own goal of skill development and accomplishment in life.

Consider another scenario, one in which envy isn't allowed to block the life-change that you seek.

Someone achieves a place in life you long for. You celebrate his achievement and seek to learn from him all that you can, drawing important lessons from his experiences and victories. Instead of an adversary, he becomes a mentor and a strategic resource. In celebrating what God is doing through his life, you gain a glimpse of what God might do someday with you. Instead of feeling insecure or threatened, you have an increased sense of development and achievement.

Few modeled this more authentically than John Wesley and George Whitefield. Friends in their earlier years at Oxford, their ministries ran on parallel tracks, with both enjoying wide acclaim. Yet envy was held at bay. Indeed, it was Whitefield who encouraged Wesley to begin his famed outdoor preaching. Upon the death of Whitefield, Wesley was asked if he expected to see his old friend in heaven. Positioned for competition because of similar venues and opposing theologies, Wesley's reply staggered his inquirer: "No, he'll be so near the throne of God that men like me will never even get a glimpse of him!"[24] The devil is "wounded to the death by love for our enemies," notes the Parson in *The Canterbury Tales,* and when the envious repent in Purgatory, no wonder Dante finds that the cords that bring them to their repentance are drawn by "charity's correcting hand."[25]

By entering into the celebration of what God is doing in another's life, you allow yourself to trust in what God has in store for your own life. By trusting in God's sovereign plan and His promise to lead you into a future of blessing, you can enjoy the security of God's love. This is the security that overcomes envy. It involves offering a radical yes to the work and wisdom of God, submitting to His choices and gifts, His dictates and maneuverings. God offers security amidst an uncertain future. But we can enjoy that peace and security only when we turn away from envy.

In heaven, we won't be looking around to see what others have or how they have been rewarded by God. Instead, we'll be filled with awe and wonder at the Gift-Giver and the wonderful providence He displayed toward us.

A PRAYER AGAINST ENVY

The best prayers are those that shape us to God's will and wisdom. They become channels of God's activity and power into our lives. The worship leaders of Israel, under King David, understood this, crafting prayers that seemed not only to express the heart of the worshiper, but then set the path of where that relationship with God needed to travel.

One such prayer captures the pilgrimage away from envy toward security in God. Its opening words are authentic and transparent:

> When I was beleaguered and bitter,
>
> totally consumed by envy,
>
> I was totally ignorant.[26]

This is the confession we need to make. Not simply of the state of envy, but that it is rooted in ignorance—ignorance of who we are, ignorance of who others are, and ignorance of the wisdom and will of God. It acknowledges the failure of envy to see life beyond these temporal shores, and past our momentary wants and desires. The deeper truth that holds the antidote to envy is knowledge of the love of God and a recognition of our own hand-fashioned nature.

> But you've taken my hand.
>
> You wisely and tenderly lead me,
>
> and then you bless me.[27]

The prayer then moves on to reflect on how God is not simply active in the lives of others, but in our own lives as well. The words remind us that God is unfolding a plan in our lives and that His plan for us is a source of immeasurable blessing and security. Throughout our lives, God is developing us, giving to us, and using us in ways that are unique to who we are. Our security lies in the distinctive nature of our relationship with God and our trust that He knows best how to accomplish His plans. Ultimately it matters not where we are led or how we are used, but *that* we are led by God and that we participate with others in the grand scheme of His design.

> You're all I want in heaven!
> You're all I want on earth!
> …I'm in the very presence of God—
> oh, how refreshing it is![28]

Then comes the affirmation that real fulfillment can be found in God alone, Who replaces a desire within us for what others have with a desire for what He wants to bring into our lives. We no longer desire what others have but what God has for us! Even more important, our hearts supremely call for God Himself. Rather than seeking the things possessed by others, we seek a Person, the Source of our security.

Corrie ten Boom was part of a Dutch family who lived above a tiny, nondescript watch shop in the small city of Haarlem. During the horrors of the Second World War, she and her family were imprisoned by the Nazis for offering safe haven to Jews.

When I first read the remarkable tale of the ten Boom family, I was struck by the incredible passion that they held for God. In spite of circumstances, in spite of pain and trial, difficulty and heartache, they were simply in love with God and thought of Him at every turn. Not since Brother Lawrence's reflections on the practice of the presence of God had I encountered such simple, daily, vibrant faith.

Corrie ten Boom, after spending time as a prisoner in Ravensbruck, the infamous Nazi concentration camp, traveled throughout the world telling her story of suffering in the context of her love for God. Such were her wanderings that she referred to herself as a "tramp for the Lord." For thirty-three years following Ravensbruck, she never had a permanent home.

When she was eighty-five years old, some friends provided her with a lovely home in California. It was a luxury she never dreamed she would have. One day, as a visitor was leaving, he said, "Corrie, hasn't God been good to give you this beautiful place?"

She replied firmly, "God was good when I was in Ravensbruck, too."[29]

And the prayer comes back in all of its fullness:

> You're all I want in heaven!
> You're all I want on earth!
> ...I'm in the very presence of God—
> oh, how refreshing it is![30]

When we have God we have everything there is. When we've given ourselves to God, we have all the gifts that He generously gives. With such riches at our disposal, what reason is there to want anything else? The security that comes through knowing God and trusting in His love leaves no room in our hearts for envy. No one else has possessions or accomplishments that will ever compare with the riches we receive from the Giver of all good things.

Reaching the Point of Enough

The Journey from Greed to Contentment

"The point is, ladies and gentlemen, that greed, for lack of a better word, is good. Greed is right. Greed works."

These words, uttered by Gordon Gekko, the financial tycoon played by Michael Douglas in the movie *Wall Street,* became a cultural symbol of the end of the twentieth century. Particularly the eighties.

We began the decade by electing a new president named Ronald Reagan, who, like many of the roles he had filled as a movie star, seemed to ride in from the range, bigger than life. When he threw a multimillion-dollar inaugural ball, with his wife, Nancy, wearing a twenty-five-thousand-dollar gown, it was like the crack of a starting gun. We all jumped in and said, "Let the good times roll." And they began to roll.

The inflation rate dropped, the recession began to loosen its grip, and jobs started to open up. During the seventies we'd been standing in line for gas, turning our thermostats down, driving smaller cars, and making sacrifice after sacrifice. During the eighties we said, "Enough of that. It's time for me." The day of self-interest had dawned.

In 1967 a survey of college freshmen revealed that 83 percent of incoming students went to college to develop a philosophy of life. By 1987 the number-one answer had little to do with anything philosophical; the average student went to college to learn how to make more money. They didn't care what they were called to do, made to do, or gifted to do. They had little concern with what was happening in the world, or the difference they could make in global affairs. What mattered was how much they'd get paid for doing something, and if it paid well, then that's the thing they wanted to do.

As a result, the number of students majoring in English declined by more than 60 percent, as did many of the other liberal arts disciplines. The number of young people majoring in business and economics more than doubled. *Money* magazine became one of the hottest-selling periodicals in the country. The television show *Dallas,* about a rich Texas family, ranked number one in viewership for the first half of the decade, only to be succeeded by *Dynasty,* about another rich family. And then, as if that weren't enough, we ogled the mansions and extravagant baubles of various celebrities on Robin Leach's *Lifestyles of the Rich and Famous.* Madonna arrived and charted a number of top hits with her "Material Girl" persona.

Our heroes weren't found among the ranks of social workers, philosophers, teachers, pastors, or scientists. Instead we revered Lee Iacocca, Donald Trump, Ivan Boesky, and Carl Icahn. Phrases like "junk bonds," "corporate raider," and "hostile takeover" entered our vocabulary. And then *Time* magazine declared 1984 the Year of the Yuppie—BMW-driving, brie-eating, Rolex-wearing, debt-accumulating machines.[1]

And incredibly, we all wanted to be one. Was Gordon Gekko actually right? Was greed really good?

Let's take a second look at the eighties. In 1986, Ivan Boesky pleaded guilty to insider trading, setting off a wave of prosecutions related to financial self-interest. On Monday, October 19, 1987, known as Black Monday, the stock market crashed, with the Dow plummeting 508 points—at that time a catastrophic drop. By 1989, President Bush had to authorize the allocation of $300 billion in public funds to prevent the collapse of the savings and loan industry. The late eighties were marked by countless bankruptcies and personal business collapses, and the hundreds of thousands of people who had built their lives on economic self-interest saw their lives crash along with their financial dreams.

Lee Atwater, not long after attaining the pinnacle of political influence, reflected on life as he faced terminal illness at the age of forty-one. "The eighties were about acquiring—acquiring wealth, power, prestige. I know. I acquired more wealth, power, and prestige than most. But you can acquire all you want and still feel empty. What power I wouldn't trade for a little more time with my family!"[2] By the end of the decade we'd learned our lesson—we realized how empty and meaningless it all was to devote our lives to the pursuit of riches.

Or did we?

The twenty-first century dawned with the sensibilities of the eighties still intact. A twenty-six-year-old woman who was newly employed at Priceline.com told *Forbes* magazine that her goal was to be "obscenely wealthy by the time I'm 30."[3] A Harvard University undergraduate who set up an Internet dating service said, "I will feel like a failure if I am not a millionaire by my twenty-fourth birthday."[4] Cuba Gooding Jr. won an Oscar for portraying a professional athlete who kept shouting at his agent, "Show me the money." Consider the widespread acceptance of life goals such as "having it all," "financial success," or "the good life." Rob Walker, writing in the *New York Times Book Review,* observed, "If Gordon Gekko were to spring to life now, who would he find to argue with?"[5] Apparently, not many. A survey conducted by the business journal *Fast Company* asked, "If you could have one more hour per day at home or a $10,000-a-year raise, which would you rather have?" Eight out of every ten respondents said, "Give me the raise."[6]

"We've got a form of brainwashing going on in our country," Morrie sighed one day. In the book *Tuesdays with Morrie,* sportswriter Mitch Albom sat at the feet of his old college professor, Morrie Schwartz, and learned some of his deepest life lessons. Diagnosed with amyotrophic lateral sclerosis (ALS), better known as Lou Gehrig's disease, Morrie welcomed his former student's weekly visits. Every Tuesday, Albom would write down what he learned during the dying man's final months. "Do you know how they brainwash people?" Morrie asked him. "They repeat something over and over. And that's what they do in this country. Owning things is good. More money is good. More property is good. More commercialism is good. More is good. More is good. We repeat it—and have it repeated to us— over and over until nobody bothers to even think otherwise."[7]

GREED AND LIFE-CHANGE

When it comes to life-change, greed would rarely be first on anyone's list. It's not that we consider greed to be good—we don't—but we hesitate to believe that it's really all that bad, either. The fruit of greed is often wealth and acquisition, two things that are universally heralded as noble goals and aspirations. But true greed is not simply the possession of things, nor is it the love of possessions. As essayist and social critic Henry Fairlie observes, it is the love merely of possessing.[8]

This is behind Jesus' most comprehensive treatment of the dangers inherent within greed's grip on a life:

> "Watch out! Be on your guard against all kinds of greed; a man's life does not consist in the abundance of his possessions."
>
> And he told them this parable: "The ground of a certain rich man produced a good crop. He thought to himself, 'What shall I do? I have no place to store my crops.'
>
> "Then he said, 'This is what I'll do. I will tear down my barns and build bigger ones, and there I will store all my grain and my goods. And I'll say to myself, "You have plenty of good things laid up for many years. Take life easy; eat, drink and be merry."'
>
> "But God said to him, 'You fool! This very night your life will be demanded from you. Then who will get what you have prepared for yourself?'
>
> "This is how it will be with anyone who stores up things for himself but is not rich toward God."[9]

Why did Jesus come down so hard on wanting more than what you have? What's the problem with seeking to accumulate a few possessions more than you have right now—isn't that what life is all about?

"No," Jesus says, "it isn't."[10]

THE HARD TRUTH ABOUT GREED

Before we can begin to break the grip of greed, we need to face some facts. There are two ugly realities associated with greed. First, it's essential that we acknowledge how attractive the lie of greed is. And second, we need to realize that greed truly determines our character, distorting our souls in the process.

Greed Is an Attractive Lie

Greed, while worshiped by many in our culture with an almost religious fervor, is antithetical to the genuine life-change we seek. First, it defeats positive change by selling us an attractive lie. Greed would have us believe that happiness is found in getting things. When we believe this, we make things, and the money to buy things, our ultimate life pursuit. Yet this pursuit is a mirage, leading us in vain to keep seeking a never-realized sense of having accumulated enough.

In his book *The New New Thing*, Michael Lewis describes the rise of Silicon Valley by telling about the life of Jim Clark, who created the billion-dollar companies Silicon Graphics and Netscape. When Clark started Silicon Graphics, he told a friend that all he really wanted was to have $10 million. If he could just reach that level, he'd be happy. Then, just before he started Netscape, he told one of the young engineers who helped him create his first company that what he'd really like to have is $100 million. Then, when he reached a personal net worth of $600 million, he said, "I just want to have a billion dollars, after taxes. Then I'll be satisfied."[11]

The numbers kept changing. But they always will, because that's how greed's subtle nature works. Greed wants you to play the "if only" game. If only I had that, then I'd be really happy. If only I could amass that much wealth, I'd be set for life. Greed paints a target on the wall that promises everything, yet delivers almost nothing. No matter how much we get, happiness and the life we long for seem to require just a little bit more, leaving us in never-ending toil to obtain what we'll never achieve. We become like Sisyphus, who according to Greek mythology was doomed forever to constantly roll a heavy stone uphill, only to see it roll back down just before reaching the top.

Jesus challenged people to realize that if they reduce life to things, and the money to buy those things, they are fools.[12] It would be difficult to imagine Jesus saying that with an edge to His voice, or in a condescending manner. It's more likely that He issued the warning in a voice tinged with sadness. Sad because of the incredible number of lives He knew would buy into the lie of greed. Sad because so many wouldn't find out until it was too late that they had wasted their lives.

Tolstoy explored this theme in a short story about a man named Pahom, whose only goal in life was acquiring things. Learning of a country where he could accumulate land for less than a penny an acre, he sold everything he owned and made his way to its borders. Upon his arrival, Pahom gave gifts to the inhabitants and asked about buying land. The chief of the people fulfilled Pahom's dream by telling him that he could have all the land he could walk around in a single day.

Embarking at dawn so he could secure the greatest amount of land, Pahom traveled farther and farther, unable to let go of a single acre. Then came the inevitable setting of the sun, forcing him to race back to his starting point in order to complete his circle in a single day. The exertion overcame him and he fell dead just as he made it back to where he'd started. As he died, Pahom looked up and saw the image of the chief turn into the image of the devil himself.[13]

The deadly lure of greed is its all-consuming nature, which directs a life away from the pursuit of God. Jesus said it well: We can't serve God while pursuing wealth and serving the purposes of greed.[14] Greed removes a person's life from the path of following God's purpose and prevents that person from experiencing God's life-directing and life-changing power. Frederick Buechner's irony-filled observation rings true: "There are people who use up their entire lives making money, so they can enjoy the lives they have entirely used up."[15]

Greed Repositions Your Heart

Greed begins by proclaiming a lie that promises fulfillment while stealing away one's life. But it doesn't stop there. The second deadening effect of greed is that it repositions our hearts.

Two of the most provocative passages in the Bible speak to this, beginning with a sobering observation directly from Jesus: "Wherever your treasure is, there your heart and thoughts will also be."[16]

Now reflect on that for a minute. Whatever you treasure, whatever you value, whatever you cherish as your ultimate goal—that is where you have placed your heart. If you've bought into the lie of greed, then you've taken your heart from its God-ordained place, which is to be turned toward God and opened to Him, and redirected it to worship instead at the altar of things. Greed, by its very nature, leads to idolatry. Greed first displaces God from His throne, then enthrones the god of money to begin its deadly rule. Since one cannot love both God and money, the heart ceases to be open to God. The effect of this is strategic, for it brings a new compass to bear that directs a life away from true north. Acquisition, not the guidance of the Word of God or the promptings of the Holy Spirit, becomes the new directing force.

Which brings us to the second provocative verse: "For as he thinks in his heart, so is he."[17] Your heart determines who you are. Everything else in your life that indicates your priorities, your passions, your allegiances, it all flows from that same internal source. The orientation of your heart does much more than simply determine your purpose; it changes your character and shapes your soul.

A few years ago many eyes were opened by the book *The Day America Told the Truth*. The book was built on a series of surveys that tried to get at what people really think and feel. In the chapter on money, it was revealed that for ten million dollars, one out of every four of us would abandon our friends as well as our religious faith. We would also become a prostitute for a week. One out of every fourteen of us would murder someone in exchange for ten million dollars.[18]

Alarming? It gets worse. The polltakers reduced the amount by one-half and still received the same results. Then they dropped it to four million, then three million. Same responses. They have no idea how low they could have gone. It almost doesn't matter, for the point had been made. It brings to mind the story of a man who propositioned a woman to sleep with him for twenty-five dollars. She absolutely refused. He upped the price to one thousand dollars. She refused again but with a bit less fervor. He kept increasing the price until he offered her one million dollars. She hesitatingly agreed.

"Just this once though."

He then said, "Well, can we make it twenty-five dollars instead?"

Offended, the woman said, "Twenty-five dollars? What kind of a person do you think I am?"

"We've already determined what kind of a person you are," the man replied. "Now it's a matter of negotiating the price."

If we let it take our heart, greed will set the agenda for who we are. Dante's many "daughters of Avarice"—listed as treachery, restlessness, fraud, perjury, deceit, inhumanity, and violence—will become our offspring, for they are sired by greed's desire. For example, writing about the success of pyramid schemes—the classic ploy to get people to give you money on the promise that by doing so they will make more money, then you tell them all they have to do is recruit their own group to do the same thing, and so on—Robert Todd Carroll notes that "pyramid schemes are popular because people are greedy and greed can do wonders to a person's thinking."[19]

The life-determining nature of greed is vividly portrayed by C. S. Lewis in *The Voyage of the Dawn Treader* when young Eustace encounters a dragon's lair filled with a dragon's rich hoard. Allowing himself to become taken with greed, he begins to stuff his pockets with treasure. Falling asleep on a pile of coins, he later awakens to the sight of a dragon's claw before his face. It was his own.

"He had turned into a dragon while he was asleep," Lewis writes. "Sleeping on a dragon's hoard with greedy, dragonish thoughts in his heart, he had become a dragon himself."[20]

THE JOURNEY FROM GREED TO CONTENTMENT

If greed really can hold us in such bondage, what hope is there of breaking its manacles? The promise of freedom comes in the form of a new heart, provided by God and oriented toward God. From the staging area of a heart opened to God's desires and seeking His will, the power and presence of God is marshaled to assault the citadel of sin. So how can our hearts be given to God in light of greed's ever-tightening grip? As with all life transformation, addressing greed is a matter of directive values and conscious decisions. Rather than seeking happiness by looking outward to money and possessions, we need to look to an inward state of the heart, the state of contentment. The Bible shows that we can arrive at this state when we adopt three new ways of viewing life.

Clarify Needs versus Desires

The first step toward contentment involves differentiating between needs and desires. It begins when we focus on what we have, not on all the things we don't have. This is easy to say, but difficult to do, for it calls us to do the hard work of separating needs from mere desires.

When my wife and I moved to Charlotte to start a new church, we had to rent a house. Buying wasn't an option. Imagine going to a bank and being asked, "How much do you make?" and being forced to reply, "Well, nothing. Yet. At least I hope it's 'yet.'" Which leads the loan officer to query, "So, where exactly do you work?" And you are again forced to say, "Well, my job doesn't exactly exist yet." Cue silent alarm that summons the security guard. So we rented a little home, just over eighteen hundred square feet, and stuffed our six-person family into its three small bedrooms. Yet we were grateful. It had so many things we loved—a large, private back yard. Good neighbors. Great location.

Before long we were able to buy a home. And not just any home, but one that embodied everything we'd ever wanted. It was a large brick colonial sitting on a heavily wooded two-acre lot. Once the papers were signed, the final months in our rental home turned unbearable. Every blemish, every defect, every cramped nuisance came to the surface. But our new house—now there we just knew we'd be happy forever.

About a year after we moved into our dream home, we innocently ventured to the Charlotte Homearama, which that year was based in the city's latest premiere golf community. The tour featured multimillion-dollar houses offering floor plans from eight thousand to twelve thousand square feet. A Jacuzzi was featured in every bathroom and a wine pantry on every floor. One home even had its own putting green in the back.

Suddenly our dream house wasn't so dreamy. Instead of seeing our new home for all that it was, we were suddenly looking at it for all that it wasn't. God had allowed us to produce a good crop, but all we could think of was an even bigger one.

To get past this brief flirtation with house envy, we remembered what we had—not in relation to those who had more but to those who had less. It was a simple maneuver but a decisive one.

I read of a family that made a commitment to support five orphaned children in Haiti above and beyond their giving to their local church, allowing the Haitian children to be fed, clothed, and educated. It meant the family would have to sacrifice. Their children had to ride second-hand bicycles, and sometimes their Christmas presents weren't the latest and most expensive must-have item available. Yet the family stayed with their commitment to the orphans for more than a decade.

One day the father learned that his company was going to be sending him to Haiti on business. He'd be able to take the entire family, enabling them to meet the five children they'd been supporting. On their second day in the country, they rented a jeep and drove out to the village where their young friends lived.

When they arrived late in the afternoon, the children were waiting in front of the school building. Having been told in advance of the family's visit, they'd been standing there since early that morning, anxious to see the Americans who had loved them so much with their gifts. As soon as the jeep stopped, the five Haitian children raced over to embrace the family, crying and weeping with joy and gratitude.

The children gave the family the only present they could afford—handmade ornaments for their Christmas tree—made of twigs and sisal. After as long a visit as they could manage, the family headed back to Port-au-Prince.

Throughout the ride back to the capital, the two American children sat in silence. The father thought that perhaps they were regretting where their family's money had gone for so many years. Was it possible that this lesson of sharing had backfired?

The father finally asked what was wrong.

"Oh, nothing's wrong," answered the daughter. "I was just thinking that there is nothing we could have done with our money over the last ten years that would have made us happier than we are now."[21]

Value Eternity More Than Earthly Riches

The second step in breaking greed's grip is to take an eternal view of life. Reflect again on the story Jesus told. God said to the man, "You fool! This very night your life will be demanded from you. Then who will get what you have prepared for yourself?"[22] Jesus calls us to see beyond this life as the end-all of our existence.

We've all had moments of truth when the real value of money and possessions is seen for what it is—or more important, for what it is not. In February 1997, Microsoft CEO Bill Gates, the richest man in America, spoke to more than a thousand people at the convention of the American Association for the Advancement of Science. After Gates's speech, Dr. John Cantwell Kiley, a medical doctor with a Ph.D. in philosophy, stood and asked a question.

"If you were blind, would you trade all of your billions to have your sight restored?"

"Yes," Gates replied. "I would. I would trade all of my money for my sight."[23]

When faced with such considerations, the words of Jesus ring true: "Watch out! Be on your guard against all kinds of greed; a man's life does not consist in the abundance of his possessions."[24] The point is that we must refuse greed a place at the table and instead pull back the chair for God to sit down. That can happen only when we intentionally take stock of money's place in relation to life itself. The life we're so familiar with is a small drop in the ocean of eternity. Material possessions and the pleasure of accumulating things bring only momentary pleasure. We need to invest in things of eternal value.

Make the Right Investments

Finally, if we're going to get past greed, we have to take the words of Jesus to heart and become rich toward God. Being rich toward God means prioritizing our life investments around Him, including our financial values and priorities. The Bible tells us there is something inherent in the act of giving that supernaturally alters who we are from the inside out, and in turn produces in our life everything we most want.

Notice the promises contained in these verses of Scripture:

"Give, and it will be given to you."[25]

"He who gives...will lack nothing."[26]

"Whoever sows generously will also reap generously."[27]

While greed repositions our heart toward the lie that "things" are everything, giving our money away repositions our heart and puts our treasure with God. When that happens, our heart follows suit, which opens the door to God and all of the life-changing power and presence He alone can bring.

Here we must be particularly on guard against the subtle nature of greed. We think of the miserly stinginess of Ebenezer Scrooge, the personification of hoarding money and refusing to care about the needs of others. This extreme characterization doesn't reflect our own disposition—few of us would ever treat others as callously for the sake of money as did Dickens's immortal character—so we relieve ourselves of the challenge to give generously.

Yet the real presence of greed remains. We see it in conspicuous consumption, which has so leveraged our resources that we aren't able to drive a stake in the heart of greed through our generous giving. Rather than changing our spending habits, we let the amount of our outstanding debt insulate us from feeling any guilt over our miserliness. "It's not that I don't want to give, or that I don't care about others," we tell ourselves. "It's just that I can't." The reason many of us can't give has nothing to do with being overextended financially; it goes back to the condition of our hearts. Many of us have spent all that we have on ourselves, leaving nothing to be given to others.

Now let's stop for a moment, because this discussion is becoming uncomfortable. Giving, lifestyle, and debt are highly personal matters, and talking about them causes our defenses to go up. Fair enough. But let's at least be honest about why we become defensive; it's because Jesus was on target in His assessment. He made it clear that the condition of your heart is revealed by the location of your treasure. If your heart desires something else more than it hungers for God, how you use your money will expose that condition. Even further, money is the great means for indulging selfish whims, and we resist anything that would encourage us to die to ourselves. So whether your heart is devoted to God or to personal pleasure is exposed as well by how you use your money.

Greed is insidious. The more money I have, the more I am tempted to make it the focus of my life, because it caters to my self-interest. Apparently, I'm not alone. *Time* magazine reported on a major study that revealed how we use our money. Those who earned less than $10,000 a year gave, on average, around 5.2 percent of their income to charity. People who earned between $10,000 and $20,000 gave only 3.3 percent. And people who earned between $75,000 and $100,000 gave only 1.6 percent.[28] The ability to give and the commitment to give are two quite different things.

I can think of three reasons it's absolutely essential that I give. First, God tells me to do it, so it's an act of submission and obedience. If my faith and relationship with Him are going to have any authenticity at all, I need to honor God's request. Second, I need to know the blessings of giving. When I give, I receive much more in return than I ever give. Third, when I give, I announce again what is true and strike a powerful blow against the lie of greed. Every time I give, I serve notice on my life and my feelings, my thoughts and emotions, and my heart and my soul about what is true. And this is the truth: Money doesn't give meaning to life. Only God has the power to do that.

Answer these three questions, and be honest: What is real, what is lasting, what is truly honored as your god? God, and only God, represents true and ultimate reality. God, and only God, is eternal, limitless, and unchanging. Finally, God, and only God, is the Creator, the Almighty, the beginning and the end. There is only one true God, and it's not money.

Acknowledging God as God and money for what it is, a tool to use in doing good for others, gives God the foothold He needs to release His transforming power in your life—even into the areas infected by greed. Only God has the power to replace your greed with His contentment. And when we allow Him to do that, our heart—and our treasure—will be in the right place indeed.

Taming the Senses

The Journey from Lust to Self-Control

If I were to buttonhole people on the street and say, "There's an ancient list based on the Bible, dating back to the fifth century, that identifies the top deadly sins. Which one do you think tops the list?" I'll bet you anything that the number-one answer, in one form or another, would be sex. This same conviction led Dorothy Sayers to title her classic moral essay "The Other Six Deadly Sins."

While most people would agree that the church historically has looked down on sex, on a personal level they don't believe sex is that big of a deal. Our culture tends to look at the Bible's standards for sexual morality and judge them passé and out of touch with the real world. Surely God cares more about poverty and disease and war than He does about what two people do in the privacy of their home. In fact, the Bible's clear requirements regarding sexual restraint are now considered a vice, or at the very least an unnecessary and unwanted encroachment on personal liberties. One father, profiled in a *Glamour* magazine article, drove his daughter and her boyfriend to a hotel for the express purpose of having this young girl lose her virginity. The title of the article, written by the boy who was dating the daughter, was "My Girlfriend's Father—What a Man!"[1]

The terminology we use to describe sexual involvement reflects a shift in the way society views sin. Sexual activity outside of marriage is no longer adultery, but "an affair." Adultery is such a negative word, after all, but an affair holds the promise of mystery, excitement, and intrigue. It's considered a relationship, not a sin.[2] Sexual content on television now shows up in two of every three programs, with only 10 percent of those depictions emphasizing anything related to sexual risks or responsibilities.[3] In such a climate, it's no wonder that a wife went to lunch with eleven other women, and when one woman asked "How many of you have been faithful throughout your marriage?" only one hand was raised. Describing the scene later to her husband, one of the women confessed that she was not the one who had raised her hand, but quickly added, "But I've been faithful to you." When her husband asked why she hadn't acknowledged her fidelity, she responded, "I was ashamed."[4] Tragically, we've arrived at the point where sexual fidelity is now the lifestyle that brings shame.

We're engulfed by a culture that contends that the way to live life to the fullest is to set free our sexual appetites, inclinations, and orientations—and in so doing, address the areas of our lives that seem to be in need. At the very least, even when we pay lip service to the importance of sexual restraint, we're ambivalent as to its urgency. This makes the inclusion of lust on the list of the deadly sins even more puzzling. Since it stops short of engaging in an actual sexual act, lust seems innocent, almost laudable for its restraint.

But something still is not quite right, even for those who hold a cavalier attitude toward lust. C. S. Lewis notes that we can easily attract a large audience to watch a woman undress on stage. But suppose you visited a country where you could fill a theatre by simply bringing a covered plate onto the stage and then slowly lifting the cover to reveal, just before the lights went out, that it contained a mutton chop or a bit of bacon. Would you not think that in that country, something had gone wrong with the appetite for food?[5]

Yes, you would.

But what the ancients sensed with lust runs deeper than simply misapplied attention to the sexual act. Drawing from Scripture and, no doubt, personal experience, they knew that lust consumes the heart and mind in sexual thoughts and attitudes that not only dishonor God but also lead to acts that dishonor God. Lust not only corrupts the heart, but as Proverbs reminds us, "For as he thinks in his heart, so is he."[6] Or as we might paraphrase the verse, "so *does* he."

THE SEXUAL LEARNING CURVE

On her grandmother's birthday, a young girl asked the elderly woman how old she was.

"Honey, when you are my age, you don't tell anybody how old you are," the grandmother replied.

"Aw, come on, Grandma. Tell me," the little girl replied.

The grandmother laughed and teasingly said, "No!"

The little girl sneaked into her grandmother's bedroom and emptied out her purse. The grandmother came up the stairs and caught the girl red-handed.

"What are you doing?"

"I'm looking for your driver's license," the girl said, "because I'm going to find out how old you are!"

"Well, all right," the grandmother said. "What does it say?"

The little girl looked at the license a minute, did some figuring in her head, and said, "Grandma, you're seventy-six years old!"

The woman said, "That's right, honey. I am seventy-six years old."

Then the girl's eyes got big. "And, Grandma, you made an 'F' on sex!"[7]

If you took a test on sex, what grade would you make? Perhaps not as high as you might think, which is why the following primer on the Bible's view of sex may be of interest.

GOD CREATED OUR SEXUALITY

First, it was God who created our sexuality. Sex was part of His desire and design for our lives, rooted in the very record of creation itself:

> The LORD God said, "It is not good for the man to be alone.
> I will make a helper suitable for him."…
>
> Then the LORD God made a woman…and he brought
> her to the man…. For this reason a man will leave his father
> and mother and be united to his wife, and they will become
> one flesh.
>
> The man and his wife were both naked, and they felt no
> shame.[8]

In this opening treatise of the Bible we have the clearest statement imaginable that God created Adam to want, need, and desire a woman: his wife, Eve. And not just emotionally, but physically. The intimacy was to be of such a nature that they would become one flesh. Sex was God's idea, God's design, and God's creation. It makes sense, then, that God's rules regarding sex would assure the optimum benefit and fullest expression of this act. Freedom in sexual expression begins with God and His design for this special act.

SEX IS A GIFT

For Adam and Eve, the pursuit of sexual intimacy carried no shame. Under God's design, sex was something blessed, never dirty or cheap, sordid or immoral. It was meant as a gift. In Proverbs, the Bible says, "Let your manhood be a blessing; rejoice in the wife of your youth. Let her charms and tender embrace satisfy you. Let her love alone fill you with delight."[9] And in one of the most overlooked books in the Bible, the Song of Songs, we find a beautiful love poem between a man and a woman, where we read words of sexual invitation and enjoyment:

> "Let him kiss me with the kisses of his mouth—for your love is more delightful than wine. Pleasing is the fragrance of your perfumes."[10]

> "My lover is to me a sachet of myrrh resting between my breasts."[11]

> "How beautiful you are, my love, how beautiful! Your eyes are soft as doves'. What a lovely, pleasant thing you are, lying here upon the grass."[12]

We could go on, but my contacts are starting to fog up.

This gift goes beyond physical enjoyment, for the intended blessing also includes intimacy. God designed sex to do something to the people who engage in it, to enact something between them. Notice what the apostle Paul wrote of this: "There's more to sex than mere skin on skin. Sex is as much spiritual mystery as physical fact.... 'The two become one.' "[13]

No other human activity has the same power as sexual intimacy. It is the supreme expression of a committed, intimate relationship. It is ultimate emotional unity. Through sex, we draw near to each other in ways unavailable through any other means.

In light of the pleasure and intimacy God designed for sex to bring, how tragic that Freud would write of a Victorian woman who, on her wedding night, drugged herself into unconsciousness, leaving a note for her husband which read, "Do to me what you must." Nothing could be further from God's intention for sexual activity in our life.[14]

Equally perverse is when sex is pursued with enthusiasm but divorced from true, lifelong commitment to one another. This is lust at its most base, for it takes the wonderful, beautiful gift of sex that God gave to men and women for their oneness within marriage and twists it into nothing more than a physical craving to be satisfied.

God designed sex to be part of the deepest nature of intimacy and community—for community is meaningful relationship and interaction with another. The reduction of sex to lust isolates it from its rightful environment, a committed marriage. Lust steals a person's value by reducing him or her to a mere object of gratification. Lust subverts the God-intended purpose of sex—a deepened marital relationship—and replaces it with the driving force of satisfying one's physical urges. Even as we tend to use the word *lust*, it's in regard to lusting *for* or lusting *after*—placing the emphasis on something or someone as an object, not a person.[15] Lust takes sex, designed by God to deliver fulfillment, and twists it into something that promises pleasure but ultimately delivers only emptiness and regret. Indeed, this is one of the great themes of the wisdom contained in the Proverbs, where time and again lust and its results—such as adultery—are seen as the road to ruin. What was pursued for pleasure produced only pain.[16]

Those who have divorced sex from its relational anchor in marriage find this to be true. One man who had been involved in numerous affairs confessed that he felt like he'd "left little bits of myself all over the place."[17] This man had entered into oneness, and the separation of the one back into two always damages the soul. That's why the Bible proclaims, "The body is not meant for sexual immorality."[18]

This is not difficult for sexually promiscuous people to intuit. The late (and never-married) NBA star Wilt Chamberlain claimed to have slept with more than twenty thousand women. Chamberlain went on to write in his autobiography that he would have traded all twenty thousand for one woman he could have stayed with forever.[19] Yet despite what we might know to be true at the end of the day, or at the end of a life, we continue to buy into the lie, so much so that when a Zogby International survey asked, "How likely do you think it is to find sexual fulfillment through the Internet?" one in four American men and about one in six women replied that it was very likely. Tragically, nearly one in five Christians agreed.[20] No wonder the business of selling sexual desire through images has become a $10 billion annual industry in the United States alone.[21]

SEXUAL FULFILLMENT IS INTENDED FOR MARRIAGE

The Bible defines sex as a creation of God that He gave to us as a gift. Then it goes further to establish that sex is designed for intimacy and fulfillment exclusively within the bonds of marriage. This excludes sex before marriage, outside of marriage, and after divorce.

The Scriptures are not ambiguous on this point. We read in the book of Hebrews that we are to "honor marriage, and guard the sacredness of sexual intimacy between wife and husband. God draws a firm line against casual and illicit sex."[22] Today that verse may need some amplification. In the first national data gathered on the sexual practices of fifteen- to nineteen-year-old males, a study financed by the federal government found that teens are confused as to what abstinence means, reducing it solely to the avoidance of genital sexual intercourse. Anal sex and oral sex seem to have the green light, falling outside the popular definition of sex. The report found that many adolescent males consider oral sex to be a substitute for intercourse and something that doesn't qualify as actual sex.[23]

The teaching of Scripture brings clarity to such confused and ambiguous understandings. Sexual intimacy, not merely intercourse, is reserved for men and women within the confines of marriage. And God has His reasons.[24]

THE DAMAGE OF SEX OUTSIDE OF MARRIAGE

We're all familiar with good things being used for a purpose they weren't intended to perform. When something is used to accomplish what it wasn't designed to do, it often brings devastating consequences. A fire within a fireplace is beautiful and brings warmth. Outside of those confines, it can destroy a family's home. Likewise sex, when it is reserved for marriage, builds intimacy between spouses. This fits its design. But that same bonding quality of sex, outside its designed parameters, can produce untold heartache.

Lust Destroys Emotional Union

If you are married and allow lust to lead to a sexual relationship with anyone other than your mate—even a fantasy relationship fueled by pornography—you are destroying the emotional union of your marriage.

Because sex was designed by God to foster intimacy and make the two one, it needs the safety and boundaries of marriage to protect it from wounding us deeply. "We must not pursue the kind of sex that avoids commitment and intimacy," the apostle Paul wrote in his first letter to the Corinthians, "leaving us more lonely than ever—the kind of sex that can never 'become one.' "[25] If you've ever talked to someone who has suffered because of a mate's infidelity, they will testify to this truth. The resulting pain wasn't just that their mate shared his or her affections with another, but the fact that they were betrayed. Dr. Frank Pittman, an Atlanta psychiatrist interviewed by *Newsweek* magazine about adultery, said it isn't about "whom you lie with. It's whom you lie to."[26]

Sex outside of marriage also can easily destroy potential emotional union between those yet to be married. No one doubts the power of sex, but consider the *consequences* of its power. Having sex when you're dating—or even engaged—can overwhelm the relationship, with physical intimacy becoming a substitute for emotional and spiritual intimacy. Sex also confuses overpowering physical sensations with feelings of love, leading many couples into marriage when in truth they are poorly suited both for each other and for the commitment required to succeed in marriage. The powerful attraction of sex can't help but dominate the relationship, not to mention the couple's feelings and their thinking. With sex in the forefront, the infrastructure needed for a lasting relationship can't be built. It's no surprise, then, that research conducted by sociologists from the University of Chicago and the University of Michigan found that couples who live together before marriage are more apt to end up in divorce court than those who wait to move in together after their vows.[27]

Lust Destroys Our Relationship with God

Second, when we give in to lust in any of its forms—either by allowing it to lead to acts of sexual sin or by simply giving it permission to control our thought life—it's a direct offense against God, and direct offenses against God have spiritual repercussions.

We want to develop ourselves spiritually. We long for intimacy with God. This close relationship with Him is integral to experiencing His power and work in our lives. But going against His sexual design separates us from enjoying intimacy with Him. It tears away at our soul and drives God away. The apostle Paul wrote about this:

> There is a sense in which sexual sins are different from all others. In sexual sin we violate the sacredness of our own bodies, these bodies that were made for God-given and God-modeled love, for "becoming one" with another. Or didn't you realize that your body is a sacred place, the place of the Holy Spirit?[28]

Lust Destroys Our Bodies

Pursuing lust and the physical activity it often leads to can destroy our bodies through sexually transmitted diseases. No, the Bible doesn't say, "Guard against the threat of venereal disease." And no, I don't believe AIDS is a plague of God's judgment against gays. Yet the Bible does say, "Can you build a fire in your lap and not burn your pants? Can you walk barefoot on hot coals and not get blisters?... Adultery is a brainless act, soul-destroying, self-destructive."[29] More than fifteen million new cases of sexually transmitted diseases are contracted every year in the United States alone. The AIDS epidemic continues to grow in many parts of the world. Public education efforts aimed at convincing people to wear condoms during sex have failed to assure the "safe sex" that was promised. The failure rate of condoms when it comes to preventing pregnancy is somewhere between 15 and 26 percent, and HIV is 450 times smaller than sperm cells.

The culprit behind the spread of sexually transmitted diseases is lust. Dr. Virginia Cafaro, an HIV specialist in San Francisco, notes that the "party scene is much more active, the sex clubs are back in bloom and the Internet is just an incredible avenue for people to meet. They go online, introduce themselves and an hour later there's a stranger at your door."

Seth Watkins, an HIV-prevention educator and counselor in San Francisco, knows the power of lust and its peril. He is infected with HIV himself. Yet despite his vocation, he fails to practice what he proclaims to others, as he continually places himself and possibly others at risk. On the night he feels he contracted the disease, he notes that "we were just so attracted to each other, and we wanted to have sex."

Yet to Jeff Getty, a founder of Survive AIDS in San Francisco who has lived with HIV for two decades, such thinking—and the activity that follows—is incomprehensible.

"I can't imagine someone being HIV [positive] and taking risks with this disease," Getty said. "This morning my back is out again, I have sciatica, I have a herpes shingle going right up my back. I'm just now finishing all my drugs. Yesterday I had to take injections to make my bone marrow grow, and my life is not fun. Sometimes I wish I were dead. If somebody was HIV negative, and I could transport them into my body for a few days and let them feel the pain, I think they'd have a whole new understanding about the risks they're taking."[30]

The Journey from Lust to Self-Control

The sin of lust would have us believe that sex is good in every circumstance and that feeding our sexual desires will bring fulfillment. Because our sexual urges are so strong, it's hard not to believe this lie. Psychiatrist Louis McBurney has observed that the path to sexual sin is often paved with the notion that feelings are not only all-important, but also totally uncontrollable. Feelings and overpowering urges just happen to you.[31] As McBurney points out, the belief in irresistible sexual urges is a false belief. It's simply not true.

No matter the situation, regardless of the circumstances, our sexual choices are just that—choices. When we find ourselves attracted to images, influences, or behaviors that would war against intimacy with our mate, would estrange us from God, and could threaten our very lives, there are four deliberate acts of self-control we can utilize that will join our choices to the power of God working in our lives.

Say No Early On

The correct answer to sexual temptation, in all its forms, is no. And the time to give that answer is when you first find yourself being lured away from God's purposes for sex. Draw the line against the earliest stirrings of lust. Be firm, definite, and unwavering. Don't allow lust to produce its offspring, sexual immorality.

For men, lust usually begins with the eyes. Men are naturally attracted to the female form, so the pornography industry has no trouble finding plenty of customers. The lure of lust through pornography is as near as the local convenience store and as quick as a click of your computer mouse. Given the prevalence of this ever-present temptation, there is only one hope for victory: the word *no*.

Consider the snare of online pornography. It seldom begins with a race to a porn site on the first day you sign up with an Internet Service Provider. Instead, it's a subtle process, beginning with curiosity that leads to gradual explorations that often lead deeper and deeper into habitual consumption, even addiction. What would have been considered unthinkable terrain just weeks earlier is now a compulsion that steals your attention, passion, and energy. Your desire for your mate, and for God, is redirected by the sin of lust.

For women, the lure of lust is usually relational rather than purely sexual. It often comes in the form of romance novels or Internet chat rooms. Women seek attention, a listening ear, someone who makes them feel beautiful and valued and cherished. If they feel those qualities are missing from their marriage, they might be tempted to seek them elsewhere—through friendship with a male colleague, for instance. And true to its character, lust exercises a gradual and growing influence over us. A woman seldom flings herself at a man, hoping to be taken immediately to bed. Instead, it begins with an enjoyable conversation, which leads to a friendly lunch, then a longer lunch, then a ride home from the office and perhaps a stop for a drink along the way. Lust pretends to offer care and attention but is satisfied with only one outcome—a full-scale sexual relationship. The doorway lust presents here is not purely sexual; it is guised in emotions. For a woman, saying a preemptive *no* to lust might have to do with the earliest stages of emotional dependence, as opposed to any physical or sexual attraction.

There is no lack of opportunity to toy with lust. But toying with this sin is like toying with a tiger. Victory demands self-control. The person being tempted must respond with a clear, unambiguous *no*. Say it clearly, say it early, and say it often. A *maybe* won't do, for lust has a strange kind of appetite—the more you feed it, the more it grows.

Be Mindful of Others

Here's a second key to conquering lust: Become intensely mindful of those you love. An act of sexual infidelity is never limited to just two people. Sexual sin devastates the lives of those closest to you. When you sense the temptation of lust, fill your mind with the faces of all the people who would be marked forever by the pain of your betrayal. Lust is an intensely selfish and self-absorbed internal sin that often leads to overt acts of sexual sin. Being mindful of the loved ones you would be hurting brings forth the light needed to banish lust beyond the borders of your life.

This strategy of considering the impact of your sin on others dates back to the early desert fathers—leaders of the earliest Christian ascetic communities—who wrote of the value of putting a "bitterness into your thought" regarding the consequences of lust, meaning to purposefully reflect on its dark and acrid aftereffects.[32] Psychologist Solomon Schimmel writes of his success in this manner with one of his patients. "By my shifting the focus of therapy from my client's and his lover's desires and needs to their moral obligations to others, he was able to end the affair."[33]

Remember God

Third, in the midst of temptation, remember God. When Joseph was confronted with sexual temptation in the famed Old Testament account, he cut to the heart of the issue, asking "How...could I do such a wicked thing and sin against God?"[34] Whatever entered his mind when Potiphar's wife threw herself at him—lust, fear, or simple awkwardness—his ultimate thought was toward God. To Joseph, God was not merely a concept. He was a Person with whom Joseph enjoyed a close relationship. Joseph knew that giving in to lust would damage his relationship with God. He also knew that God was not kept out of a room simply because the door was shut. God was real, God was there, and God would see everything if Joseph were to agree to the seductress's evil invitation.

Today we're confronted with the same invitation to lust that Joseph faced. And never before has the invitation to sexual sin been so enticingly private. The Internet offers at least forty thousand sex-oriented sites that are available in the privacy of your home.[35] No longer do you have to enter a store to rent a video or DVD to feed your private fantasies. The inhibiting risk of public humiliation or discovery has been eliminated. As one father who was wrestling with the implications of Internet porn wrote, "I found my first porn in the woods by some freakish accident, and it was many years before I saw anything like it again. My son had it delivered to him in the family room, where he was able to see it whenever he wanted, as often as he liked."[36] Never before has an awareness of God's presence been more critical. While the public will never know if we indulge in cybersex, God will always know. So given the pervasiveness of pornography, we must recall the Bible's words: "the LORD sees clearly what a man does, examining every path he takes."[37]

Set Up Barriers

The only person who knows you better than you know yourself is God. So partner with God to conduct a personal inventory. Ask God to help you develop a healthy sense of your own areas of weakness and vulnerability, and then take steps to compensate for them. "As a bodyguard is always standing by to protect the Emperor," writes desert father Abba Poemen, "so the soul ought ever to be ready for the demon of lust."[38] Because the "demon of lust" is crouching just about everywhere these days, we need to have protective barriers in place to shield us from temptation. Anticipate the assault and protect yourself in advance. The worst thing you can do is assume you don't need to take precautions, thinking you can handle whatever might come along. You can't, and neither can I.

The only hope for success is to acknowledge that we are weak and vulnerable creatures. The quicker we own that, the better off we'll be, so let's get real nuts and bolts about it, beginning with current relationships:

Do you look forward to appointments with a particular member of the opposite sex?

Would you rather spend time with this person than with your spouse?

Do you seek to meet with this person away from your office in a more casual environment?

Do you prefer that your coworkers not know you've set up another meeting with this person?

An affirmative answer to any of these questions should be considered a warning light.[39] You need to establish barriers immediately. Eliminate any interaction with this person that you can. If you are counseling the person, refer him or her to someone else. If you're working together, ask to be moved to another project.

Similar barriers are needed in other areas of sexual temptation. If you can't stay away from Internet porn sites, move your computer to a heavily trafficked area of your home, install filtering software, subscribe to a family-friendly Internet Service Provider, or simply get off of the Net. If late-night cable gets to you, end your subscription. I know of people who, whenever they travel, unplug the television, and of one man who insists that the television be removed from his hotel room. Other friends make sure they take along pictures of their wife and children, and they keep the pictures by their bed.

Those who fight lust and win have a "whatever it takes" mentality. Early on in his life, a lanky North Carolina farm boy with aspirations to make an impact for God gathered his ministry team around him in Modesto, California, and hammered out their Modesto Manifesto, committing themselves to financial integrity, moral purity, working with the local church, and honesty in all matters related to publicity.

Their commitment had teeth. For example, from their resolve for moral purity came boundary lines. They wouldn't travel alone, they would share hotel rooms, they wouldn't counsel a woman alone. Their commitments mattered. We've seen leader after leader drive their lives into a moral ditch. But not this man or anyone on his ministry team. His name? Billy Graham. As a result of Graham's choices made years ago, God gained a servant He could use to change the world.

THE GREAT MIND GAME

The Bible speaks of taking every thought and making it captive to the Word of God—and through this, being transformed by the renewing of our minds.[40] This is the essence of the battle against lust.

Author and pastor John Claypool tells of two Buddhist monks who were walking just after a thunderstorm. They came to a swollen stream, where a young woman stood waiting to cross to the other side. She hesitated to cross alone due to her fear of the swift currents.

One of the monks asked if he could help, and the woman agreed to be carried across the stream. The monk put her on his shoulder, carried her through the swirling waters, and put her down on the other side. He and his companion then continued on to the monastery.

That night his companion said to him, "I have a concern about your behavior. As Buddhist monks, we have taken vows not to look on a woman, much less touch her body. Back there by the river, you did both."

"My brother," answered the other monk, "I put that woman down by the other side of the river. You're still carrying her in your mind."[41]

Lust is a mind game. What we nurture within our mind journeys straight to our heart. The prevailing wisdom behind all of the strategies to combat lust, which allow God to renew our minds and then transform our lives, is to leave whatever we might pick up along the way by the side of the river, and then move on.

And to do it at once.

Turning Away from Self

The Journey from Pride to Humility

In 1978, when Reggie Jackson rejoined the New York Yankees after serving a five-day suspension for defying orders from his manager, Billy Martin, an army of sportswriters attended his return. Standing in front of his locker, a reporter asked the slugger what thought was uppermost in his mind during the suspension.

"The magnitude of me," Jackson replied.

Fast forward to another professional athlete named Reggie. In 1995, the season before the Green Bay Packers won Super Bowl XXXI, Reggie White—the team's defensive captain as well as an ordained minister—learned that a reporter was experiencing terrible pain in his right knee.

"I'll pray for you," said the All-Pro defensive end.

The sportswriter assumed White meant that he'd pray next Sunday in church. Instead, Reggie went to the locker room and came back with a teammate, Keith Jackson, along with a jar of ointment. Reggie dabbed a little cream on the man's forehead, and then he and Keith—a combined

558 pounds of NFL muscle—knelt and prayed aloud for the reporter and his knee.

That's a tale of two Reggies,[1] as well as a tale of contrasts between two spirits.

C. S. Lewis writes that there is one vice of which no person in the world is free, which everyone in the world loathes when he sees it in someone else, and of which hardly any people, except Christians, ever imagine that they are guilty themselves.[2] That vice is pride.

Most of us have a sense of what pride is all about, and we know that in many ways it can be a good thing. We want to take pride in a job well done. We talk about being proud of our children. But we also know pride has a dark side, where appropriate levels of self-esteem give way to self-love. If I were to say, "He's a prideful person," you'd picture someone whose arrogance and conceit push others away.

One such woman led off an ad in the personals section of *New York* magazine with the words "Strikingly Beautiful" and then described herself as "Playful, passionate, perceptive, elegant, bright, articulate, original in mind, unique in spirit. I possess a rare balance of beauty and depth."[3]

Kinda makes you want to puke, doesn't it?

But there's more to the dark side of pride than simple vanity. That is a mere caricature of this sin. Vanity is a relatively benign trait that reduces self-absorption to lingering glances in the mirror and gratuitous boasts inserted into conversation. Yet vanity masks the real pitfall of pride, which is the idea that we can produce from our own imagination, our own resources, or our own insights the standards and guidelines by which we will live. It's placing ourselves above any other source or authority that might speak to who we are, what we believe, or how we should live. We assume the position of authority because we don't think anyone or anything else is truly superior to us. It's for this reason that Dorothy Sayers remarks that pride is one of the few issues in life that attacks us not on our weak points but on our strong ones.[4] It plays to what we think we can do, what is biggest and best within us, which leads us to look down on everyone and everything else. The more competent we consider ourselves to be, the more prideful we tend to become. When our sense of ability, knowledge, or skill is believed to equal or surpass that of others, we refuse all counsel but our own.

Dante shared this assessment, so much so that when he painted his picture of the proud of heart in his fictitious portrayal of hell, he presented pride as men and women who carry huge stones on their backs that bend them over so they can't see anything but the ground. Since they looked down on everyone else in life, they were now unable to look up to see anything at all.[5]

CONFUSING OURSELVES WITH GOD

It was this blight on the soul that led the ancients to designate pride as not only one of the deadly sins, but marking it as perhaps the *most* deadly. "We are talking," observes essayist and social critic Henry Fairlie, "about someone who cannot be reached."[6] Perhaps even more tellingly, the victim of pride is someone who doesn't feel the *need* to be reached. Thus pride sets the soul on course to attain a single pursuit—the establishment of self as God.[7]

It was through the prophet Ezekiel that God traced this inevitable sequence of events: "In the pride of your heart," God warned, "you say, 'I am a god.' "[8] To be "a god" is to be self-determining and self-governing. It yields no quarter and bends no knee. There can be no equals, only rivals.

And it possesses a strong, almost irresistible, allure—even to those who deny the idea of deity itself. No less a figure than Bertrand Russell, famed author of *Why I Am Not a Christian,* confessed his attraction to this idea, writing "Every man would like to be God."[9]

It was this very thing that led to the downfall of Satan himself. The Bible reveals that Satan was one of the greatest of angels, but chose to enter into rebellion against God. Notice Isaiah's record of his fall:

> How you have fallen from heaven, O morning star, son of the
> dawn!… You said in your heart, "I will ascend to heaven; I
> will raise my throne above the stars of God; I will sit
> enthroned on the mount of assembly, on the utmost
> heights.… I will make myself like the Most High."[10]

Through the prophet Ezekiel, God added these words regarding Satan's demise: "Your heart became proud on account of your beauty, and you corrupted your wisdom because of your splendor."[11]

Pride is the seedbed of rebellion against God, because it chooses to cast God from His throne and place another in His place—namely *ourselves.* Pride is, by its very nature, competitive.[12] And if not competitive, then most certainly exclusive. It will happily remove itself from any and all situations in which an outsider might challenge it or assert authority over it. As Milton imagined Satan declaring, "Better to reign in Hell, than serve in Heaven."[13] C. S. Lewis was right when he said pride is the complete anti-God state of mind.[14]

A KING DESTROYED BY PRIDE

Few of us deliberately nurture pride. We don't issue an open invitation for it to come and take residence in our lives. Instead, pride takes root gradually, after its initial appearances simply go unrecognized. We compare ourselves to others constantly, and the more we come through the process with our egos intact—finding fault with others, sensing our own "superiority"—the more our pride is enhanced. We don't tell ourselves we are better; we simply give in to the feeling of satisfaction that we don't share another's weakness. Thus we give in to pride's seductive embrace, slowly at first, but then with increasing abandon, until its hold on our lives becomes obvious to everyone but ourselves.

A similar progression marked the life of a man named Uzziah, an obscure king whose story is tucked away in the annals of the Chronicler, but whose reign provides one of the most incisive case studies of a life consumed—and eventually destroyed—by pride.

Uzziah's fall truly was tragic, because at the start he had it all. Raised in prominence and privilege, his father was the king of Judah. At sixteen years of age, Uzziah ascended to the throne. The early years of his rule were marked by an authentic devotion to God. The teenager proved to be a prodigious leader and began to enjoy unprecedented success.

But the king's great strides weren't his own. The Bible notes that "as long as he [Uzziah] sought the LORD, God gave him success."[15] Sadly, Uzziah failed to see the connection. He began to attribute his success to his own skills and abilities rather than the workings of God, and thus began his descent into the pit of pride. As noted, pride takes control gradually. The beginning indulgences of vanity give way to the initial acceptance of personal credit for what in truth is God's work. This leads to the burgeoning belief in superiority, giving way to a blinding embrace of self-sufficiency.

Uzziah was textbook.

Early faithfulness to God was usurped by pride's unchallenged march through his life. No longer would others be allowed to speak to his soul. Now, *he* would do the speaking. In the end, he even took it upon himself to enter the temple of the Lord and conduct worship for himself, unconsecrated and in violation of God's laws regarding the priestly service. Pride had such control over him that he took it upon himself to become his own priest.

When confronted by a courageous Levite who was aghast at the king's sacrilege, Uzziah broke into a rage that his self-primacy would be challenged. But what broke out on Uzziah was leprosy. The priests, seeing the clear judgment of God, hurried their king out of the temple. One can't help but smile at the Chronicler who noted that upon the sudden affliction, "he himself was eager to leave."[16]

Subsequently forced from his throne, Uzziah lived the remainder of his life with the disease in an isolated house and was eventually buried in a nearby field, separated from kings who had gone before him. In setting himself above others in self-ascribed glory, he sealed his fate to be laid low in self-inflicted shame.

According to the Bible, he lost everything because of a single factor: "his pride led to his downfall."[17]

This same virulent strain of pride, Cornelius Plantinga observes, is still with us. Professors leave faculty meetings feeling less enlightened by what they heard than by what they themselves said. People take offense when they receive praise that falls short of what they feel they deserve. What has changed, says Plantinga, is that in much of contemporary American culture, "aggressive self-regard is no longer viewed with alarm. Instead, people praise and promote it."[18] We reside in what Christopher Lasch termed a "culture of narcissism."[19]

Earlier generations of saints saw the danger and sounded the warning.

When asked to name the three primary precepts of Christianity, reformer John Calvin dryly replied, "I would answer, 'Humility.' "[20] Why? Augustine provides the answer: "Pride is the beginning of sin."[21]

THE JOURNEY FROM PRIDE TO HUMILITY

Imagine if at every turn in your personal history you could go back and give God His proper place in your life. If you could go back and give Him honor where it was due. If you had rightly acknowledged that He alone was on the throne instead of trying to force Him aside so you could take His place. If you had followed where He had called, obeyed where He had asked, embraced His wisdom and insight. What would that have done for you? There can be little doubt in anyone's mind as to the staggering scope of what might have been.

In the movie *The Family Man*, Nicolas Cage plays Jack Campbell, a successful player in the marketplace who is happily living his single life. He has everything he desires, or so he thinks. One day he wakes up to a different life, one in which he didn't abandon his college sweetheart for a job in London. In this new life, he is married to his old flame, has two kids, and makes a living selling tires at Big Ed's. At first, Jack desperately wants his old life back. But then, day by day, he senses what he has been missing. In the reverse of *It's a Wonderful Life*, Jack realizes what his life could have held if he had only made more virtuous choices.

We cheat ourselves out of the excitement of being a part of God's work because we're not willing to seek His leading, listen to His voice, and then follow His lead no matter where it takes us. We mistakenly believe that a self-directed life will lead to fulfillment and personal glory. If only we knew where such a course actually leads and, in contrast, where the path to true glory and significance can be found. A path where our steps would join with God's, and the destination would be everything we longed for.

The path of humility.

Yet how can we move from pride toward humility and begin to create the foundation for the life we're called to live? The heart of the Bible's wisdom and insight is captured in a single verse: "Do not think of yourself more highly than you ought, but rather think of yourself with sober judgment."[22] In that admonition to the Christians living in Rome, we find the key to defeating pride and developing humility: honest, realistic self-appraisal. It involves coming to know exactly where we stand in relation to reality.

I once read of a ship's captain who looked into the dark night and saw faint lights in the distance. The distant lights held steady and gradually grew stronger. They followed a direct collision course with the ship. Immediately the captain told his signalman to send a message: "We are on a collision course, advise you change course twenty degrees."

Promptly a return message was received: "Advisable for you to change course twenty degrees."

The captain was incensed; his command had been ignored. He fired off a second message: "I'm a captain. Change course twenty degrees."

"I'm a seaman second class," came the reply. "You had better change course twenty degrees."

Furious, the captain sent a third message: "I'm a battleship. Change course twenty degrees."

Then the reply came: "I'm a lighthouse."

I believe it's safe to assume that he changed course.[23]

This is the way sober judgment manifests itself. It's the lighthouse of humility that addresses the battleship of our ego. However, unlike the young seaman, it doesn't send a direct message our way. Instead, sober judgment must be cultivated within our souls in three very specific areas: honest self-assessment, an accurate recognition of God, and submission to the discretion of God.

Sober Judgment Assesses Our Strengths and Weaknesses

First, sober judgment must be allowed to do its work in accurately assessing our personal strengths and weaknesses. Okay, we can see the relationship between weakness and the virtue of humility. But strengths? What's the connection?

Humility has nothing to do with denying our strengths or trying to pass them off as something they're not. It's not about a pretty woman pretending to be ugly, or a smart person believing he's a fool.[24] The foundation of humility is *truth*. The authentically humble person sees himself as he is—nothing more and nothing less.[25] God gave your strengths to you, so it would be wrong to try to deny them. Humility doesn't pretend that we don't possess the obvious strengths that God has given us.

Mark Van Doren, a literature professor who once taught Thomas Merton, visited his former student at a Kentucky monastery after a thirteen-year separation. "Of course he looked a little older," Van Doren recalled, "but as we sat and talked…I interrupted a reminiscence of his by laughing. 'Tom,' I said, 'you haven't changed at all.' "

"Why would I?" replied Merton. "Here our duty is to be more ourselves, not less."[26]

Authentic humility calls upon accurate knowledge of who you are and the active pursuit of becoming who God intends you to be. Just as Thomas Merton learned in the monastery, we all need an honest awareness of our personal strengths and giftedness if we are to become the people God created us to become.

But soberly assessing our strengths is only half of the personal inventory that humility requires. The other half is much more difficult to submit to. Sober judgment possesses full knowledge of our weaknesses and deficits, our inadequacies and needs. It is the recognition of our less noble attributes that stirs resistance within the deepest recesses of our souls. This is where we see pride warring against humility, and humility struggling to disarm the power of pride.

Sociologist Erving Goffman has rightly identified our attempts to live as con artists, convincing others and ourselves that we are something we're not. Doctors can try to inspire awe in their patients by pretending to be able to diagnose what they really don't understand. Lawyers can pretend to know exactly what the law allows when in reality their knowledge is quite limited. Teachers can present themselves to their students as owning more knowledge than they really possess.

Sober judgment refuses to indulge such self-deceit. Thus, humility prevents the failure that comes from trying to be what we are not and trying to perform what we really don't know how to do.[27] When such sober judgment reigns in our lives, the door is opened for the rare gift that flows solely from the wellspring of humility—*wisdom*.

There's a legend about the great wisdom of the Greek philosopher Socrates. The Oracle of Delphi pronounced that no one in the world was wiser than Socrates. This puzzled the great sage, for he didn't consider himself to be wise at all. So Socrates commenced a journey, seeking out all who were purported to be wise to determine if indeed he was the wisest of all. Time and again he discovered that those thought to be wise were not, yet they always *believed* themselves to be. Socrates came to the conclusion that the Oracle pronounced him the wisest man in the world because he alone knew that he was not. Humility made him the greatest intellect on earth.

In this spirit, Robert Morneau writes that humility is "that habitual quality whereby we live in the truth of things: the truth that we are creatures and not the Creator; the truth that our life is a composite of good and evil, light and darkness.... Humility is saying a radical 'yes' to the human condition."[28]

Owning up to our weakness carries far more worth, however, than correct self-assessment. It is through our own sober judgment that God can confront us with our sin and demonstrate our need for repentance. If you refuse to admit the truth about yourself, you won't face up to those facets of your life that need to be changed. Instead of owning mistakes and confessing wrongdoing, your tendency will be to fault others or blame your circumstances. This is why the one great spiritual disease is thinking yourself to be without fault. Only when you can own your broken condition can you turn toward the transforming presence and work of the living God. As reformer John Calvin reflected, "When anyone realizes that in himself he is nothing and from himself he has no help, the weapons within him are broken, the wars are over."[29]

Sober Judgment Knows Who God Is

Having sober judgment that identifies the truth about oneself is only one dynamic of humility. A second pursuit must be the clear realization of who God is and who *isn't* God.

Think about your top strengths and your best abilities. Sober judgment knows that they come from God. Humility refuses to even entertain the idea that they are somehow a result of our own cleverness or effort. For example, Billy Graham—known for his self-deprecation—was once asked why God chose to use him throughout the world to introduce people to God. The evangelist responded, "That's the first thing I'm going to ask Him when I get to heaven."[30]

When we achieve something, earn something, or create something, humility knows that it was, in the final analysis, a *God* thing. It refuses to give in to the idea that we somehow did it on our own, or that we are unique and irreplaceable. As the apostle Paul wrote to the Christians in Corinth:

> [Do not] take pride in one man over against another. For who
> makes you different from anyone else? What do you have that
> you did not receive? And if you did receive it, why do you
> boast as though you did not?[31]

When it comes to assessing our accomplishments and successes, humility knows that the honor and glory go to God. Humility doesn't give in to the temptation to think that somehow we truly deserve the accolades because of some inherent superiority that we possess.

When it comes to life choices, deciding what to do or how to live, humility knows that it must turn to God and submit all plans, all value judgments, all courses of action to Him. Humility knows that no one else can, or should, lead us in life. It would be folly to even flirt with thinking otherwise, because there is a God and we are not He.

Thus, sober judgment leads to the one thing pride can't bring itself to yield: the bended knee. True worship—not the synthetic type that seeks a cheap emotional high, but true worship that seeks to elevate God and bestow honor and praise independent of self—is that which drives pride from our lives. Once it flees, true life-change begins. The bended knee is the one force that opens our hearts to God's transforming power.

Sober Judgment Submits to the Discretion of God

Finally, sober judgment has a servant's heart that submits to the discretion of God.

There is much to be gleaned from the simple admonition from Jesus to sit at the back until called forward, rather than assuming that the place of prominence has been saved for you. Unchecked pride can fuel an ambition that seeks out acclaim, reaches for status, and positions itself for notoriety. Such exaggerated self-regard can translate into a quest for recognition and prominence.

Submission to the discretion of God is captured in the life of the person Jesus mantled as the greatest figure to date in human history—John the Baptist.[32] A contemporary of Jesus, a blood relation, and acclaimed as the prophet of his day, John was prime material for pride. Yet when confronted with what God was doing through Jesus, John simply noted, "He must become greater; I must become less."[33]

Precisely what pride does not wish to allow.

We are driven people, wanting to succeed, to accomplish, to be known. We are easily seduced by achievement and position. As Gordon MacDonald once reflected, we will fly across the country to deliver a talk but not walk across the street to hear one. We turn our backs on God's words through the prophet Jeremiah: "Should you then seek great things for yourself? Seek them not."[34]

But what of ambition? Isn't that a virtue, particularly when it is devoted to advancing the kingdom?

Jim Collins, former Stanford University professor and now director of a management research laboratory, separates personal ambition from selfless ambition through a discussion of what he calls Level 5 leadership, the highest level of effectiveness for building enduring greatness. Collins writes that "Level 5 leaders channel their ego needs away from themselves and into the larger goal of building a great company. It's not that Level 5 leaders have no ego or self-interest. Indeed, they are incredibly ambitious—*but their ambition is first and foremost for the institution, not themselves.*"[35]

This is the distinction between noble ambition for the kingdom of God and prideful ambition for the glory of self. Rather than the self-oriented pursuit of a personal vision or a life of individual fulfillment, the path toward humility surrenders such things to God with a servant's heart. It does not seek its own agenda but rather the agenda of the kingdom of God. We are called to live large but not to be large ourselves. The more I reflect on the writings of the great figures throughout Christian history, the more I see this mark on their lives. They were fueled not by accomplishment and acclaim but by a desire to be faithful to God and charitable toward others. Indeed, recognition—as a concern—was repugnant to them.

TAKING GOD'S PATH ON THE JOURNEY

So what would a truly humble person look like today? If we were to meet this individual, he wouldn't be what most of us would call "humble." Instead, you'd describe him as a cheerful, happy sort who took a surprising interest in what *you* had to say. As C. S. Lewis notes, the truly humble person wouldn't even be thinking about humility, because he wouldn't be thinking about himself at all.[36]

But can such a journey be made?

Hans Christian Anderson writes of a proud teapot—proud of her porcelain, long spout, and wide handle. She did not talk about her lid, for that had a crack and a chip, but she secretly prided herself on the humility of acknowledging its presence.

One day the teapot fell. Her spout broke, her handle cracked. The cups and the cream jug and the sugar bowl all laughed at the teapot. The very next day she was given to a beggar woman.

Convinced this could never be lived down, the teapot sank into a deep depression.

Yet the teapot learned that one can be one thing and then become something quite different.

Dirt was placed inside of her, and a flower bulb was planted in the soil, becoming her heart. She had never had a heart before. It brought life and power, and from that life and power, a green shoot emerged. From all of the life and thoughts and feelings came a flower.

The teapot forgot herself for the glory of the flower, and she had never been happier.

One day the teapot heard people say that the flower deserved a better pot. They cracked her across the middle, took the flower, and threw her into the yard. A broken piece here, an old chip there.

The teapot didn't care, for the flower had a better home.

And it was the flower that mattered.[37]

The Search for a Centered Soul

The Journey from Sadness to Joy

C. S. Lewis wrote movingly about his search for joy—something he intuitively knew to be distinct from both happiness and pleasure. Throughout his life, beginning with childhood, there would be arrows of joy shot at him—through strains of music, the smell of an orchard, or the grand Norse tales. But they were not joy itself. They were pointing him on to something more, something deeper, something even more real.

When he was young, Lewis didn't connect joy with God. He thought joy was best symbolized by a place, not a Person. Indeed, he feared that if there was a God, He might demand the rejection of any and all joy. Later in his spiritual journey, however, Lewis discovered that nothing could be farther from the truth. In fact, he later characterized his journey to Christian faith with the image of being "surprised" by joy in the Person of God.[1]

GOD'S CALL TO JOY

When the birth of Jesus was announced to the shepherds, the angel proclaimed, "I bring you good news of great joy that will be for all the people. Today in the town of David a Savior has been born to you; he is Christ the Lord."[2] Shepherds were poor people, often outcasts, yet joy had been announced to them. After the angelic declaration, and after the shepherds had gone to see the Baby, they remained poor and outcast. But they hadn't lost the joy that was promised.

The Bible's characterization of joy is distinct from happiness. The word *happiness* is derived from the word *happen* or *happening,* indicating that happiness occurs when things are going my way. As a result, happiness comes and goes. It's here one minute and gone the next. For this reason, John R. W. Stott notes that those who pursue happiness never find it.[3]

Joy is different. In his dictionary of theological terms, Millard Erickson writes that the biblical definition of joy is sincere satisfaction and deep delight that is *not* affected by circumstances.[4] Real joy is found in living above one's circumstances, for joy is not the absence of problems but the presence of God. It's not the removal of suffering, but the reality of God in the midst of pain and difficulty.

ON THE ANCIENT SIN OF SADNESS

Within the *Institutes* of John Cassian, by which the original list of deadly sins first entered the West, both "dejection" and "accidie"—the "heaviness or weariness of heart"—are included.[5] During the sixth century, Pope Gregory the Great modified the original grouping into a defined list of seven, folding vainglory into pride and weariness into sadness. Soon the seemingly vague sin of sadness was replaced with the more specific sin of sloth. But the assimilation of Cassian's discourses under the category of "sloth" fails to capture the "sin of the spirit" that the early monastic movement sensed within this designation. Cassian's concern over a spirit of dejection that destroyed the steadfastness of the heart was not only warranted, but critical.

For it was that which went to war against joy.

When we think of sadness or a dejected spirit, we think of it in general, almost superficial terms. The sadness that comes with grief or a sense of loss. The inclusion of sadness with the list of deadly sins reminds us that dejection of the spirit can subvert virtue and prevent us from experiencing the life-change that God wants to produce in us. Some years ago, John R. W. Stott was asked about his impressions of some of the church and seminary audiences he had addressed. Sensing the ancient category of Cassian, he said if there was one thing he wanted to say to these seminarians, it was "Cheer up! It's not that bad!" Stott had been overwhelmed by the unwarranted despondency he felt from their spirits.

The early church fathers viewed such spiritual despondency as a plague on the soul. Such a condition springs "from the desire of some gain" that had not been realized, or a plan gone awry.[6] The spirit of sadness could also flow from a sense of woundedness from a perceived affront or from a hypercritical appraisal of life.

Another of Cassian's concerns deserves the greater engagement and restoration, for it can only be related to what we would call depression. Cassian writes of that which comes upon us "without any apparent reason," finding ourselves "suddenly depressed with so great a gloom that we cannot receive with ordinary civility the visits of those who are near and dear to us."[7] This "weariness or distress" of heart is likened to a "fever" which seizes us.[8] It is here that Cassian was at his most prescient.

According to the World Health Organization, 340 million people around the world suffer under depression's weight, with 19 million of those sufferers in the United States.[9] A study published in *American Psychologist,* the official journal of the American Psychological Association, revealed that one-third of all Americans say they once felt on the verge of a nervous breakdown or had a mental health problem. The study also found that some form of mental illness will strike an estimated 50 million Americans during their lives.[10]

The Christian community has struggled with how to respond to depression. There's a thin line separating depression as set forth by the ancient listing of sins and depression as a legitimate mental illness, particularly when the outward mark of depression is often deep feelings of sadness. We all feel a little "down" from time to time. Close friends and loved ones die, relationships end, jobs are lost, children try our patience and sap our energy. Further adding to the complexity is that people often seek a pharmaceutical solution to a supposed chemical imbalance when a more accurate diagnosis would call for a steadfast spirit in deeper intimacy with the Holy Spirit, for not all despondency has a physical cause.

Yet great figures throughout Christian history have been gripped in the icy clutches of what can only be called clinical depression. In 1527, reformer Martin Luther, who penned the words to "A Mighty Fortress Is Our God," wrote, "For more than a week I was close to the gates of death and hell. I trembled in all my members. Christ was wholly lost." Luther would add that "the content of the depressions was always the same, the loss of faith that God is good and that he is good to me." Charles Spurgeon, the dynamic preacher behind the nineteenth-century revival movement, told his congregation in 1866 of his struggle: "I am the subject of depressions of spirit so fearful that I hope none of you ever get to such extremes of wretchedness as I go [through]."[11] Famed missionary Hudson Taylor battled severe depression all his life. At one point, as discovered in an unpublished note in the Taylor papers, he even contemplated "the awful temptation" to "end his own life."[12]

Despite the historical evidence of those whom God used despite their battle with depression, it's an unwritten axiom that modern Christians shouldn't struggle with emotional problems. This is the most subtle and insidious form of the "health and wealth" gospel that declares that God guarantees our health and prosperity as a divine right through our salvation. In this perspective, Christ's atonement provides total healing for the body and mind just as it offers forgiveness for the sins of the soul. This teaching is a lie.[13]

Depression is one of four diseases that physicians call mood disorders.[14] Just as diabetes has to do with a body's failure to regulate blood sugar, mood disorders result from the brain's failure to regulate the chemicals that control mood. Specifically, nerve cells in the brain communicate with each other by releasing chemicals called neurotransmitters. Norepinephrine and serotonin are the two neurotransmitters involved in depression. When there is an ample supply of these neurotransmitters available to stimulate other nerve cells, one typically feels "normal."

In depression, fewer of these neurotransmitters are released because the first nerve cell reabsorbs them before they've adequately stimulated other nerve cells. Antidepressant medicines work by increasing the amount of norepinephrine or serotonin.

Researchers have discovered that many factors, including life circumstances and genetic makeup, can bring on depression. Any combination of genetic predisposition or emotional trauma can initiate the chemical changes in the brain that cause depression. Even long, sustained seasons of stress can trigger its presence.

Studies have found depression to be more physically and socially disabling than arthritis, diabetes, lung disease, chronic back problems, hypertension, and gastrointestinal illnesses. The only medical problem found to be more disabling was advanced coronary heart disease. The U.S. Department of Health and Human Services reports that individuals who have suffered both emotional illness and cancer report that their emotional illness caused them greater pain.[15]

But sometimes depression isn't brought on by physiological causes or even extended periods of loss or life stress. Sometimes the condition has a spiritual component. Psychologist and author Larry Crabb writes that efforts to treat a psychological disorder might, in reality, "cheapen the mysterious battle raging deep" within a soul.[16] Crabb adds, "Suppose that many of the struggles we assume are symptoms of a psychological disorder are in fact evidence of a disconnected soul...a soul starving for life, then connecting with a source of life, not professional treatment, is called for."[17]

Crabb raises the same concern the early church fathers seemed prompted to try to address: a willful depression of the soul that is allowed to lead to despair. While the early fathers did not have access to the idea of chemical imbalances, the despair that was termed "sadness" in their early listing of the deadly sins was more akin to a depression of *faithlessness*. It's an unchecked emotional state that denies God's care and provision.

Consider a young Dutchman who came to Christ and went to Belgium as a missionary to work among poor coal miners. His passion for evangelism was stoked through the preaching of such luminaries as Dwight

L. Moody and Charles Spurgeon. Each day he read from his two beloved devotional books, Thomas à Kempis's *The Imitation of Christ* and John Bunyan's *The Pilgrim's Progress*.

Then two events severely challenged his faith. First, he was denied the hand of his cousin in marriage. Second, the Dutch Consistory dismissed him from his missionary work. From these events, he chose to abandon institutionalized religion, not to mention his faith in God. His faith couldn't overcome the rejection and failure. In the end, he committed suicide. Such was the tragic life of Vincent van Gogh.[18]

How can the faith of joy be sustained in the face of setback and failure, difficulty and pain? Let's look at another life that met hardship and faced depression and despair, only with a radically different outcome. Let's learn important lessons from the prophet Elijah.

A DEPRESSED SAINT

Elijah was perhaps the most celebrated and revered of all Old Testament prophets. He lived during a time of great political and social unrest. It was also a time when people were chasing after false gods, worshiping idols, and dabbling in religions and spiritual pursuits that had little to do with God Himself. God chose Elijah to be His spokesperson, His representative, His prophet to these rebellious people.

Elijah had quite a run. God empowered him to call for rain to end for three years, and then to start up again—simply by voicing the words. During a famine he touched a jar of flour, and miraculously it never went empty. He touched a jug of oil, and it never ran dry. He even raised a young boy from the dead. But the climax came on Mount Carmel. There, Elijah went head-to-head with the prophets of the false god Baal. Today, a dramatic spiritual confrontation of this magnitude is the stuff of fantasy, presented mostly in the movies. But for Elijah, it was real life.

He said to the people and to the king of Israel, "Okay, you've come to think that this Baal is god. I say that the Lord is God. So let's settle it. Get everyone in Israel together, and let's meet on Mount Carmel.

"Then we'll get two bulls, cut them up for a sacrifice, but we won't burn them ourselves. We'll each pray to our respective God to do the burning for us—even though there's four hundred and fifty of you and only one of me."

And they said, "Deal."[19]

The prophets of Baal went first. They called on their god from morning to noon, but nothing happened. Then they danced around the altar, but nothing happened. They shouted and screamed and cried out, "Baal, answer us!" Nothing happened.

Let's pick up Elijah's story in 1 Kings:

> At noon Elijah began to taunt them. "Shout louder!" he said.
> "Surely he is a god! Perhaps he is deep in thought, or busy,
> or traveling. Maybe he is sleeping and must be awakened."
> So they shouted louder and slashed themselves with swords
> and spears, as was their custom, until their blood flowed.
> Midday passed, and they continued their frantic prophesying
> until the time for the evening sacrifice. But there was no
> response, no one answered, no one paid attention.[20]

Then Elijah repaired the altar of God, one that the people had abandoned and let fall into disuse. He arranged the wood and laid the bull on it. He poured water on the wood to make sure it was soaked—three times—so that no one could accuse him of tricks or deceit.

> [Then] the prophet Elijah stepped forward and prayed: "O
> LORD, God of Abraham, Isaac and Israel, let it be known
> today that you are God in Israel and that I am your servant
> and have done all these things at your command. Answer me,
> O LORD, answer me, so these people will know that you, O
> LORD, are God, and that you are turning their hearts back
> again."
>
> Then the fire of the LORD fell and burned up the sacri-
> fice, the wood, the stones and the soil, and also licked up the
> water in the trench.
>
> When all the people saw this, they fell prostrate and cried,
> "The LORD—he is God! The LORD—he is God!"[21]

Elijah then ordered the people to seize the prophets of Baal and put them to death for their blasphemy. Before Israel's leader, the idol-worshiping King Ahab, could do anything in response, God miraculously transported Elijah to another city. All in all, not a bad day for a prophet.

As you would imagine, Ahab was none too pleased upon hearing of the day's events. Neither was his wife. Her name was Jezebel. *The* Jezebel, the one whose name is used as a euphemism for evil, treachery, and deceit. She sent a simple message to Elijah: "You're a dead man."

Now, after all the miracles God had wrought through this prophet, you'd think that Jezebel's threat wouldn't even register on Elijah's radar screen. God had enabled him to stare down the prophets of Baal and the entire idol-worshiping nation of Israel. God had demonstrated His unbelievable power through this lone prophet. So of what concern was this little threat from one angry woman? For Elijah, it was a major concern.

Notice how he responded: "Elijah was afraid and ran for his life.... He came to a broom tree, sat down under it and prayed that he might die.... Then he lay down under the tree and fell asleep."[22] It is here that sadness reared its head, for at this moment Elijah moved beyond exhaustion, beyond fear, and entered into the realm of despair. He needed God's remedy, so what did God prescribe?

THE JOURNEY FROM SADNESS TO JOY

God didn't criticize His servant for a lack of faith or ridicule his fear of the vengeful Jezebel. Instead, God prescribed a three-step solution to the problem of despondency. The same regimen that worked for Elijah can deliver us from our struggles with the temptation to a sadness that comes from a lack of faith.

Restoring Joy Through Physical Rest
The first thing God provided to initiate Elijah's recovery was rest.

> All at once an angel touched him [Elijah] and said, "Get up and eat." He looked around, and there by his head was a cake of bread baked over hot coals, and a jar of water. He ate and drank and then lay down again.
>
> The angel of the LORD came back a second time and touched him and said, "Get up and eat, for the journey is too much for you." So he got up and ate and drank.[23]

God didn't expect Elijah to immediately snap out of his condition. Instead, He took steps to care for the prophet's physical needs. Depression can be brought on by too much work, too little sleep, or a poor diet. God knew Elijah was tired and hungry. So God fed him, and then put him to bed.

One wouldn't normally think of physical rest and nourishment as being a spiritual investment to ward off the temptation to despair. Yet God knew that physical weakness can lead to spiritual vulnerability. Satan knows it too. This was why the tempter came to Jesus in the wilderness at the moment of His physical weakness and attempted to use food as the tool of spiritual destruction.[24]

We are physical creatures. To separate our spiritual lives from our physical lives is theologically unsound. Indeed, the Bible goes so far as to say that God "grants sleep to those he loves."[25] Too often we don't take advantage of this gift.

Dr. Martin Moore-Ede wrote a book called *The Twenty-Four Hour Society,* in which he describes a society that never sleeps, never quits, and never stops. His findings are blunt and to the point: We are not built for the world we have made, because it ignores the law of our limits. We need our sleep, and if we don't get it, our bodies will break down.[26]

And, I might add, so will our souls.

Restoring Joy Through Spiritual Intimacy

Once God attended to Elijah's physical needs, He proceeded to step two. After Elijah awakened from his sleep, God gave him further instructions:

> "Go out and stand on the mountain in the presence of the
> LORD, for the LORD is about to pass by."

> Then a great and powerful wind tore the mountains apart
> and shattered the rocks before the LORD, but the LORD was
> not in the wind. After the wind there was an earthquake, but
> the LORD was not in the earthquake. After the earthquake
> came a fire, but the LORD was not in the fire. And after the
> fire came a gentle whisper.[27]

God was in that whisper, coming to Elijah to address his spiritual condition. This was the second step in the prophet's restoration. Once his physical needs were addressed, it was time to address the needs of his soul. So what did God prescribe? Time with Him.

Communing with God wasn't meant to be a big, dramatic thing. Yes, there was wind, earthquake, and fire. But God wasn't in those powerful forces of nature. Those were reflections of God, but it wasn't where God would be found. He was to be found in the stillness, in the quiet, in the silent movement of His Spirit. Elijah needed to know that as important as his activity for God was, it wasn't as important as spending time with God Himself. Elijah needed real time with God, and that could only come when the prophet quieted himself enough to hear God whispering to the innermost parts of his being.

I'm reminded of reading of a traveler who once took a long journey to Africa, where he had recruited some local tribesmen to assist him in carrying his loads. The first day they moved fast and went far. But on the second day, the tribesmen refused to move. They just sat and rested. The traveler, who wanted to get on with his journey, asked them why they wouldn't keep going. They told him that they had gone too fast on the first day, and that they were now waiting for their souls to catch up with their bodies.[28]

If you're feeling depressed, God wants to meet you there. He wants to fill your soul with His presence, with His very Being, to touch you and engage you at your deepest level. But it will only come when you slow down enough to hear His whisper and then stop long enough to be with Him. This is the idea behind the words to the song recorded in Psalm 46: "Be quiet and know that I am God."[29] The words "be quiet" mean to "let go," to "cease," to "stand still." It speaks of stopping long enough to focus on God and hear what He might be saying. The book of James tells us, "Come near to God and he will come near to you."[30] But first you have to come near, which is why times of prayer and silence and solitude, times when you take the Bible and read it and reflect on it, matter so much to your emotional health.

But these times are few for us moderns.

In the movie *Nell*, Jodie Foster plays a young woman whose mother dies. Nell grows up alone in a forest, divorced from the world and its influences. She is then taken into town by well-intentioned people who believe she needs to be transitioned into the world from which she has been isolated.

As the movie develops, Nell's fate is placed into the hands of twelve jurors. After lawyers from both sides finish their closing arguments, Nell herself addresses the jury in the primitive speech she learned as a young child.

"Yo' ha' erna lay," she begins.

"You have big things," a woman translates.

"Yo known'n erna lay."

"You know big things."

Then, leaning toward the jury, gripping the rail that separates them, she says, "Ma' you'nay seen inna alo'sees."

"But you don't look into each other's eyes."

Then the intensity of her voice rises. "An yo'aken of'a lilta-lilt."

"And you're hungry for quietness."

Taking a breath as she seemingly searches for the right words, Nell continues. And her words are translated:

> "I've lived a small life. And I know small things. But the quiet
> forest is full of angels. In the daytime there comes beauty. In
> the nighttime, there comes happiness. Don't be afraid for Nell.
> Don't weep for Nell."

And as author Ken Gire has observed, Nell is right. We shouldn't weep for her; we should weep for ourselves. We have big things, we know big things, but we're hungry for quietness.[31] Apart from time set aside for God, and quietness to hear His voice, joy has very little soil from which to grow and sustain its life. In these silences, God replenishes our soul and provides us the emotional and spiritual sustenance we need. That is what combats the kind of sadness that is ours to refuse and leads to the life-changing joy we hunger for.

Restoring Joy Through Community

God has met Elijah's need for nourishment and rest, and He has appeared to the prophet in a very personal way, through the gentle whispered voice. But God still isn't finished with the process of restoring Elijah's joy.

God tells the prophet, "Go back the way you came, and go to the Desert of Damascus. When you get there, anoint Hazael king over Aram.

Also, anoint Jehu son of Nimshi king over Israel, and anoint Elisha son of Shaphat from Abel Meholah to succeed you as prophet. Jehu will put to death any who escape the sword of Hazael, and Elisha will put to death any who escape the sword of Jehu."[32]

One of the things that had drained Elijah emotionally and made him vulnerable to despair was being alone. He had no support, no encouragement, no one to stand by his side or to watch his back. He felt like he was waging spiritual battle all by himself. So God provided what the prophet needed. He said to Elijah, "Let's bring some folks into your life who will help you do what I've called you to do."

This step of the solution to sadness runs counter to our modern bent of self-reliance. It makes us uncomfortable to acknowledge that we can't succeed on our own, that we need the assistance and partnership of people of faith, people who will encourage our trust in God. We may not want to admit it, but we need others in our life. It's a lie that we can do life on our own. If we don't have some folks who walk with us, taking the same journey we're on, attempting to do what we're doing, we won't make it. At least not very far, or for very long. And when the tough times come, we need people by our side more than ever.

A young woman in our church experienced the horror of breast cancer. After it was first discovered, it was considered advanced enough to require a radical mastectomy. She and her husband quickly were surrounded by prayer and support, phone calls and meals, and all the counsel and advice their network of medical friends and family could provide. When I would try to call their home, it would take hours to get through. The line was continually busy with calls from concerned friends. When I went to visit her husband in the waiting room during her surgery, I passed three members of the church in the hospital parking lot.

On a Wednesday night, at one of our midweek services, I spoke with her husband, and he simply said, "I can't imagine going through this without a church family. It would be so lonely." That's the loneliness that God enabled Elijah to avoid. That's the loneliness that can bring on sadness, and the loneliness that is addressed by living in community with fellow believers. Part of the journey back to joy involves traveling with fellow Christians. God put Elijah back into community with those who would strengthen him. We need to ask God to lead us to a community of faith that will help us reclaim the joy of the spiritual life—and be willing to take the steps He provides.

THE JOY-FILLED LIFE

Real joy is not found apart from God. It is a cultivated, nurtured spirit that draws its life from the reality of, and a relationship with, God. It is the deepest nature of faith.

By the time this book is published, the cancer that attacked another one of my friends will have taken her life. She has inoperable, terminal cancer that began in her lung and quickly spread throughout her body. Understandably, there is little happiness in her life. Despair has tempted her at every turn. So she reaches daily for life in the face of her death, and she finds it by grasping onto the hand of God.

This past Sunday she lingered to see me following our final morning service. Her short hair, gamely attempting a comeback from the final, desperate rounds of radiation and chemotherapy treatments, has turned gray. I always look forward to seeing her. She never takes more than she gives.

That day she told me she knows where she's going. She knows her journey will bring her to a better place, a place where Jesus will welcome her arrival and embrace her in love. As tears filled her eyes, she added, "But it's hard. Sometimes I want to stop fighting." She doesn't just mean the cancer; she means the despair. But she does fight it—day by day. She spends time with God, who holds her tenderly in His arms. She is encircled by friends. She remains faithful and true to her husband and to her children.

Because of God, this terminally ill young mother of two is the most joy-filled person I know.

A Final Word

The Perfect Storm

I am not ashamed of the gospel, because it is the power of God

for the salvation of everyone who believes: first for the Jew, then for the Gentile.

For in the gospel a righteousness from God is revealed,

a righteousness that is by faith from first to last.

—*ROMANS 1:16-17*

Those two short, simple verses often are seen as the summation of the deepest, most theological book in the New Testament. And what do we find at the heart of this weighty tome? Nothing less than dramatic, transforming life-change. The power of God at work to bring about an eternal difference in an individual's life.

Paul begins his summation by going straight to the heart of the matter: the gospel of Jesus Christ. Our modern use of the word *gospel* is based on the Anglo-Saxon "god-spell," which means "God story." We use the word to translate the Greek word *evangellion*, which is where we also get the word *evangelism.* It means "good news" and refers to the message of Jesus Christ to the world: that salvation is offered to all who believe in God's Son, Jesus, as their Lord and Savior.

Paul was not ashamed of this message of good news, a particularly important word of encouragement for his readers in Rome, a city where power and image, prestige and position were everything. Here was the biggest and most advanced city in the world, a cosmopolitan city that had heard and experienced all the wisdom and knowledge that was circulating in the known world. Yet Paul was proclaiming good news involving a thirty-three-year-old Jew who was put to death as a criminal on a cross. In sophisticated Rome, it would be ironic that this story was characterized as a good thing. But Paul knew better than to feel any awkwardness over the seeming inconsistencies in his joyful proclamation.

Rome had the power of her military, the power of her wealth, and the power of her learning, but was singularly lacking in spiritual power. Revealed in the gospel of Jesus was the very power of God, a power of which Rome had been unaware.

In describing the ultimate potency of the gospel, Paul had six Greek words at his disposal. He chose the word *dunamis,* from which we get the English word *dynamite.* This is the same word used elsewhere in the New Testament to describe the power of Jesus' miracles. This word for *power* denotes a force that flows from within, from innate ability. *Dunamis* is not a power that is bestowed by some other source; it's the inherent power that resides in something by virtue of its nature. The gospel, Paul proclaimed, is God's power resulting in salvation for the one who believes. The power of God resides within the gospel.

Another look at Paul's summation reveals that there is no definite article in the original Greek wording. This is significant, because it doesn't say that the gospel is *the* power of God, but *a* power of God. It's not something that God uses from time to time. It is, in itself, a power. It doesn't simply bring power; it *is* power, energized by the Holy Spirit Himself.

And Paul wasn't just spouting a new theory. He had witnessed the gospel's power at work—not just in his own life, but in the life of person after person, in city after city. This gospel he proclaimed was not a worldview, a philosophy, or an argument that one tried to win. It was the very power of God unleashed in a person's life. A power that, if embraced, would make that person right with God. A power that would transform the person from within.

POWER UNLEASHED

In October 1991, a storm of epic proportion was born in the Atlantic. All the elements came together to create the most powerful storm ever seen in recorded history. Striking just off the coast of Gloucester, Massachusetts, it was really three storms in one: a hurricane, a flow of energy from the Great Lakes, and a frontal system sweeping through New England. It created an almost apocalyptic situation in the Atlantic, with boats encountering waves of one hundred feet—as high as a ten-story building.

The storm claimed the lives of many people, including six men aboard a fishing boat named the *Andrea Gail.* So awesome was the force and impact of this storm that it eventually spawned a book and then a movie carrying the name given it by the National Weather Service—*The Perfect Storm.*[1]

There is a similar vortex of forces that converge in the life of a Christian. These forces bring together everything that is needed to produce a moment of mind-boggling eternal impact: the message of the gospel, the power of God, and a human soul. But rather than taking lives, this "perfect storm" saves them. The elements come together for the very salvation work of God and the advent of the life-altering process of becoming like Jesus. This is life-change at its most authentic.

Sadly, many people settle for pseudo-transformation, mere cosmetic enhancements that mimic life-change, but that bear the markings of the Christian subculture more than true holiness. Equally innocuous is a life filled with knowledge and insight, but divorced from experience and application. It is the outward trappings of life-change, but without the power of God.

The promise of the gospel is complete transformation. Through God's power, we have victory over sin. Life-change means being more like Jesus today than you were a year ago. And it's not just a promise, but a reality.

Just ask Billy Moore.

William Neal Moore grew up in a tough city in Ohio. He and his friends would smoke dope and get drunk and break into bars. They committed all kinds of theft. Then Billy joined the army and got married. It wasn't long before his wife left him and took their child with her. He was broke, and he was desperate.

One night he and a friend were drunk and high and talking about how broke they were. His friend said, "I know about a guy who lives near here, and the word is he doesn't trust banks. He keeps all his money in his bedroom."

Billy said, "Is he some big, tough guy?"

The friend answered, "No, he's an old guy. Wouldn't hurt a fly."

The plot hatched in Billy's mind. He went back to the army barracks, got his gun, and drove to the man's house. The seventy-seven-year-old man was in the bedroom as Billy broke in the front door. The man grabbed a shotgun he used for hunting. As Billy entered the bedroom, the man pointed his shotgun and pulled the trigger. The aim was high, sending buckshot over Billy's shoulder. Billy took his gun, pointed it at the man, and pulled the trigger. Twice. The elderly gentleman fell dead.

Billy rifled through his victim's pockets, ransacked the bedroom, and walked away with $5,600. He fled to his trailer in rural Georgia.

It didn't take long for the police to track Billy down. Caught with the proceeds from the crime, he admitted his guilt and was sentenced to death.

Billy Moore's mom was a Christian, and she knew a Christian couple who lived near the prison. She called them and said, "I've got a son, and he's been arrested for murder. Would you please go visit him?" The couple did visit Billy, and they told him, "Jesus is willing to give you a fresh start and a new chance at life."

Billy looked at them dumbfounded. "You got to be kidding me. Don't you realize my situation here? I murdered an old grandfather. My life is over. There are no new beginnings for me."

But that Christian man looked back at Billy Moore and said, "No, you don't understand. Jesus Christ loves you so much He wants to find a way to make your life count." Billy not only heard the words of this concerned couple, but he also saw Jesus in them. He said later, "Nobody ever told me that Jesus loved me. Nobody ever told me Jesus had died for me. It was a love I could feel. It was a love I wanted. It was a love I needed."

And so Billy Moore, as hopeless and broken an individual as you could ever find, got on his knees and said, "God, I'm sorry for all I've done, and I want to live for you. If you would adopt me and take me to heaven, that would be the best. I don't have much time left, but if you could do something to make my life count, it would be like icing on the cake."

Jesus heard that prayer.

There was a bathtub on death row. Permission was granted from the guards to fill it with water. Billy Moore knelt in the tub, and the man and woman who led him to Christ dipped him backward into the water to baptize him.

Then God began to change Billy. He had been sentenced to death, but the criminal justice system is slow. It took sixteen years of living in a cage waiting to die, but during those sixteen years Billy opened his life up to God, and God changed him from the inside out.

Billy Moore became a model inmate, so much so that the guards called him "the peacemaker." Death row was an ugly, violent, hate-filled place until Billy got there. But Billy started having Bible studies with the other inmates, and one by one they found redemption and new life in Jesus Christ. Some churches sent people to visit Billy to be counseled by him. He even won the forgiveness of the family of his victim. Death row, a place that had been awful and violent, became a place of hope where people cared for each other.

In August 1990 the court system finally caught up with Billy. The hours were ticking down to August 22, when he would be executed. He was put in the deathwatch cell. His lawyers called him, but it was a strange experience for them. "We would call to console him," one lawyer later reflected, "but he ended up consoling us. Billy would say things like, 'Are you guys okay? I know this is difficult for you. Can I pray for you?' We were trying to reach out to him, and he was reaching out to us."

On August 21, 1990, just seven-and-a-half hours before Billy Moore was to be electrocuted, something amazing took place. The Georgia Pardon and Parole Board held an emergency hearing about a model prisoner they'd heard about from such spiritual luminaries as Mother Teresa, who had personally lobbied on his behalf. His head and right calf had already been shaved to receive the electrodes. But then the five members of the Pardon and Parole Board looked at that repentant, transformed man and did something so unprecedented that it made the front page of the *New York Times*. They looked at Billy Moore and said, "We're going to show you mercy." They threw out his death sentence and set the gears in motion to release him from prison. It was the first time in history that a confessed killer on death row was set free.

Today, Billy Moore is a pastor in Rome, Georgia.

Author and pastor Lee Strobel interviewed Billy. He knew what was behind Billy's transformation, but he wanted to hear him express it. "Billy, you tell me. What changed Billy Moore?"

"I'll tell you plain and simple," the convicted murderer replied. "It was Jesus Christ. He changed me in ways I could never have changed myself. He gave me a reason to live. He helped me do the right thing for a change. He gave me a heart for other people. And, Lee, He saved my soul."[2] That's the story of God and His power as written in the life of Billy Moore.

GOD, THE GIVER OF LIFE

As we have noted, the ancient list of deadly sins initially included eight, with sadness being one that later was dropped. In many ways, however, the despondency that tempts us away from trusting God still belongs on the list. As Christians examine their lives in light of the deadliest sins, they begin to feel a sense of despondency. They know God intends life to be much more than their sinful condition, and the despondency sometimes causes them to give up hope that they will ever rise above sin's grip. A fatalism develops that can put an end to any chance of future spiritual growth.

This is why the power of the gospel—not sadness over sins past and present—must be the final word. Lasting life-change is not something that comes from our own determination or self-discipline but that which depends on what is outside of us. Life-change is the work of God in us.

The destructive force of the deadly sins is not to be taken lightly. But the power of sin is no match for the onslaught generated by the coming together of God's "perfect storm"—which is the Almighty God working through the message of the gospel to redeem and transform a living soul. The long night's journey into day is just that—the life-changing journey that brings us finally into God's light and delivers us from the darkness of sin into a life of holiness. A living human soul is never the same after an authentic encounter with this power.

Just ask Billy Moore.

Notes

Epigraph

1. Thomas Merton, *New Seeds of Contemplation* (New York: New Directions, 1961), 44-5.

Introduction

1. Eugene Peterson, *The Wisdom of Each Other* (Grand Rapids, Mich.: Zondervan, 1998), 29; also adapted from Philip Yancey, *Reaching for the Invisible God* (Grand Rapids, Mich.: Zondervan, 2000), 19-20.

2. Bill Phillips, *Body for Life* (New York: HarperCollins, 1999), 1-2.

3. Henry Fairlie, *The Seven Deadly Sins Today* (Notre Dame, Ind.: University of Notre Dame Press, 1979), vii.

4. Karl Menninger, *Whatever Became of Sin?* (New York: Hawthorn Books, 1973).

5. John Medina, *The Genetic Inferno: Inside the Seven Deadly Sins* (Cambridge, England: Cambridge University Press, 2000). Medina does see, however, a place for human response to the emotions.

6. Steven Schwartz, *The Seven Deadly Sins* (New York: Gramercy Books, 1997), xi.

7. Dorothy Sayers, "The Other Six Deadly Sins," in *The Whimsical Christian* (New York: Macmillan/Collier Books, 1987), 157.

8. Ron Rosenbaum, *Explaining Hitler: The Search for the Origins of His Evil* (New York: Random House, 1998), 389.

9. Fairlie, *The Seven Deadly Sins Today,* 17.

10. Mark Twain, *Pudd'nhead Wilson's New Calendar,* xxvii, which first appeared as a series of witticisms used as epigrams at the beginning of each chapter of the book *Pudd'nhead Wilson, a Tale.* They were so popular that Twain continued the practice at the beginning of each chapter of *Following the Equator* (1897), reprinted through Dover Publications, 1989, and citing them from *Pudd'nhead Wilson's New Calendar.* See also Os Guinness, *Steering Through Chaos: Vice and Virtue in an Age of Moral Confusion,* ed. Virginia Mooney (Colorado Springs, Colo.: NavPress, 2000), 16.

11. C. S. Lewis, *The Screwtape Letters,* rev. ed. (New York: Macmillan/Collier, 1982), xiii.

12. 1 John 1:8.

13. M. Scott Peck, *People of the Lie: The Hope for Healing Human Evil* (New York: Simon & Schuster/Touchstone, 1983).

14. These confessions were made online at http://www.notproud.com, a Web site founded by Scott Huot and G. W. Brazier and designed to gather and showcase the confessions of the world in an anonymous online dumping ground for sin. The confessions are indexed by the seven deadly sins, along with a "Misc." category for indeterminate vice.

15. Cass Sunstein, *Republic.com* (Princeton, N.J.: Princeton University Press, 2001).

16. Jeremiah 17:9.

17. Philip Shenon, "Spy Suspect Known for Devout Faith," *Charlotte Observer*, 25 February 2001, sec. 1A, 18A.

18. This is also the original order, established by Gregory, maintained throughout the Middle Ages and followed by Dante and Chaucer. There are numerous treatments of the seven deadly sins, approaching the material from varying angles and dispositions. Among the best are Fairlie, *The Seven Deadly Sins Today;* Guinness, *Steering Through Chaos,* which provides both an introduction and a collection of readings; Sayers, "The Other Six Deadly Sins"; and Solomon Schimmel, *The Seven Deadly Sins: Jewish, Christian, and Classical Reflections on Human Psychology* (Oxford, England: Oxford University Press, 1997). On sin itself, see Cornelius Plantinga Jr., *Not the Way It's Supposed to Be: A Breviary of Sin* (Grand Rapids, Mich.: Eerdmans, 1995).

19. See Thomas Aquinas, *Summa Theologica,* 2a.2ae Q84.3.

20. Plantinga, *Not the Way It's Supposed to Be,* 14.

21. Maxie Dunnam and Kimberly Dunnam Reisman, *The Workbook on the Seven Deadly Sins* (Nashville, Tenn.: Upper Room Books, 1997), 2.

22. J. G. Davies, *The Early Christian Church: A History of Its First Five Centuries* (Grand Rapids, Mich.: Baker, 1965), 227-8.

23. Henry Chadwick, *The Early Church,* vol. 1 of *Penguin History of the Church* (1967; reprint, New York: Penguin, 1990), 181.

24. The originator was surely Evagrius, a fourth-century monastic, to whom the ancient list of eight can be traced. Cassian was a student of Evagrius. See John Cassian, *The Monastic Institutes: Consisting of "On the Training of a Monk" and "The Eight Deadly Sins": In Twelve Books,* trans. Jerome Bertram (London: Saint Austin Press, 1999).

25. As cited by Fairlie, *The Seven Deadly Sins Today,* 12. Gregory's main exposition can be found in *Moralia in Job,* 31.45.

26. In the late thirteenth century, the medieval sage Dante Alighieri saw such merit in the classification that he used the list to form the basis of his famed exploration of the human journey to salvation, *The Divine Comedy,* popularizing the weightier treatments of the sins that had been given by Thomas Aquinas (see Aquinas, *Summa Theologica,* II.ii). Not to be outdone, John Peckham, the Archbishop of Canterbury, soon ordered every priest in England to share the list of sins with the people at least four times a year and to be sure to do it "in the vulgar tongue" and without "any manner [of] subtlety or curiosity" to ensure they were understood (see Fairlie, *The Seven Deadly Sins Today,* 12). The listing of deadly sins was seized again by Chaucer in the fourteenth century for his renowned *Canterbury Tales,* going so far as to say in "The Parson's Tale" that these seven areas were the trunk of the tree from which everything else branched (Geoffrey Chaucer, "The Parson's Tale," *The Canterbury Tales,* ed. W. W. Skeat, sequence by Thomas Tyrwhitt, in *The*

Great Books of the Western World, ed. Robert Maynard Hutchins [Chicago: Encyclopaedia Britannica, 1952], 22:510). Building off Chaucer's literary license, Edmund Spenser attempted to characterize each sin as a person in *The Faerie Queene,* hoping to reveal the presence of these sins even more tellingly in daily life.

27. Simon Chan, *Spiritual Theology: A Systematic Study of the Christian Life* (Downers Grove, Ill.: InterVarsity, 1998), 72.

28. Gabriel Garcia Marquez, *One Hundred Years of Solitude,* trans. Gregory Rabassa (New York: Knopf, 1995).

29. Chan, *Spiritual Theology,* 73.

30. Colossians 3:5,8.

31. It should be noted that the sequence of the following chapters does not conform to the sequence of the original listing of the deadly sins. While there was some significance to the ancient ordering, particularly in listing pride first as the worst and most prevalent of the sins, there was freedom in the listing, which has been exercised in the ordering in this work.

Chapter 1

1. Adapted from Ross E. Milloy, "In Texas Prison Town, Even Freedom Follows a Ritual," *Charlotte Observer,* 24 December 2000, sec. 10A.

2. C. S. Lewis, *The Screwtape Letters,* rev. ed. (New York: Macmillan/Collier, 1982), 11.

3. Ephesians 1:1, emphasis added.

4. Ephesians 2:19, RSV, emphasis added.

5. Ephesians 3:8, RSV, emphasis added.

6. Ephesians 6:18, emphasis added. See also Ephesians 1:18, NIV, and Ephesians 4:11-12, RSV.

7. I acknowledge my indebtedness to Bill Hybels for the ideas contained in his small group study guide *The Real You: Discovering Your Identity in Christ/Interactions Small Group Series* (Grand Rapids, Mich.: Zondervan/Willow Creek Resources, 1996).

8. Adapted from Tony Campolo, *Who Switched the Price Tags?* (Waco, Tex.: Word, 1986), 195-6.

9. Ezekiel 36:26.

10. C. S. Lewis, *Mere Christianity* (New York: Macmillan, 1952), 63.

11. Geoffrey Wainwright, "Sanctification," in *The Westminster Dictionary of Christian Theology,* ed. Alan Richardson and John Bowden (Philadelphia: Westminster Press, 1983), 521.

12. See Hebrews 12:14.

13. See Alfred D. Chandler Jr. and James W. Cortada, ed., *A Nation Transformed by Information: How Information Has Shaped the United States from Colonial Times to the Present* (New York: Oxford University Press, 2000).

14. An excellent introduction to the biblical idea of knowledge is found in E. D. Schmitz's article on the Greek term for knowledge, *ginosko,* in Colin Brown, ed., *The New International Dictionary of New Testament Theology,* vol. 2 (1976; reprint, Grand Rapids, Mich.: Regency Reference Library/Zondervan, 1986), 392-409.

15. Psalm 46:10.

16. Matthew 7:23.

17. 2 Corinthians 5:21, NKJV.

18. James 2:19.

19. Adapted from Borden Parker Bowne, *The Immanence of God* (Boston: Houghton Mifflin, 1905), 29-30.

20. Colossians 2:7, TLB.

21. So how far can this process of sanctification go this side of the kingdom? Most Christian theologians embrace Luther's conclusion that we can never escape being *simul iustus et peccator* ("simultaneously righteous and a sinner"), though they join with Calvin in holding out hope that the Christian can make demonstrable progress. As a result, sanctification is past, present, and future. Past, for it begins positionally through Christ's finished work on the cross. Present, in that there is a process involved in cultivating a holy life. Future, for only in the return of Christ and the final establishment of His kingdom will the effects of sin be fully removed.

22. Dallas Willard, *The Divine Conspiracy* (New York: HarperSan-Francisco, 1998), 35-59.

23. Thus coupling the ancient insights dating back to Aristotle and *The Nicomachean Ethics* with the power and work of the living God.

24. See C. S. Lewis, *The Abolition of Man* (New York: Macmillan, 1943), 87-8.

25. See Richard F. Lovelace, *Dynamics of Spiritual Life* (Downers Grove, Ill.: InterVarsity, 1979), 103.

26. The actual wording of the first two steps, as they appear in the Alcoholics Anonymous *Big Book* from Alcoholics Anonymous World Services, Inc., is "1. We admitted we were powerless over alcohol—that our lives had become unmanageable," and "2. [We] came to believe that a Power greater than ourselves could restore us to sanity."

27. John 3:6, CEV.

28. Ephesians 5:18. The translation "be being filled" is based on the verb being a present imperative.

29. Lewis, *Mere Christianity*, 153.

30. John R. W. Stott, *Authentic Christianity*, ed. Timothy Dudley-Smith (Downers Grove, Ill.: InterVarsity, 1995), 205.

31. 1 Thessalonians 5:19, NCV.

32. Lewis, *Mere Christianity*, 72.

Chapter 2

1. The information on rage and its resulting violence is adapted from Julie Sevrens, "Management Crisis of the Moment: Anger," *Charlotte Observer,* 29 October 2000, sec. 4E.

2. Frederick Buechner, *Wishful Thinking: A Theological ABC* (New York: Harper & Row, 1973), 2.

3. Proverbs 14:17.

4. For the medical dynamics of anger, see Jerry Newcombe and Kristi Newcombe, *A Way of Escape* (Nashville, Tenn.: Broadman & Holman, 1999), 110.

5. Mark 3:1-5, Phillips.

6. Adapted from the online archives of the Salvation Army (http://www.salvationarmy.org/heritage); Cyril Barnes, *Words of William Booth* (n.p.: SP&S Ltd., 1975); and Philip Yancey, *What's So Amazing About Grace* (Grand Rapids, Mich.: Zondervan, 1997), 254.

7. John Chrysostom, homily 10, quoted in Os Guinness, *Steering Through Chaos: Vice and Virtue in an Age of Moral Confusion,* ed. Virginia Mooney (Colorado Springs, Colo.: NavPress, 2000), 116.

8. Proverbs 29:11.

9. Adapted from John Maxwell, *Developing the Leader Within You* (Nashville, Tenn.: Nelson, 1993), 142.

10. Adapted from Tony Campolo, *Seven Deadly Sins* (Wheaton, Ill.: Victor, 1987), 55.

11. Ephesians 4:26.

12. On her thesis, see Deborah Tannen, *The Argument Culture: Moving from Debate to Dialogue* (New York: Random House, 1998).

13. Carolyn Thompson, "Sandbox Altercation Makes It into Court," *Charlotte Observer,* 8 March 1996, sec. 8A.

14. John 16:33.

15. Chris Thurman, *The Lies We Believe* (Nashville, Tenn.: Nelson, 1989), 48.

16. William Richard Ezell, "Controlling the Fires of Anger," *Pursuit* 7, no. 4 (March 1999): 22.

17. Luke 6:45, MSG.

18. Seneca, "On Anger," *Moral Essays,* trans. John W. Basore (Cambridge, Mass.: Harvard University Press, 1928), 1:341. See also Solomon Schimmel, *The Seven Deadly Sins* (Oxford, England: Oxford University Press, 1997), 104.

19. Ecclesiastes 7:9, NASB.

20. James 1:19.

21. The "ABC" approach is more accurately termed Rational Emotive Behavior Therapy, and one need not embrace all of Albert Ellis's applications of the approach, much less his wide range of psychological convictions, to appreciate the way it supplies a framework for applying biblical insights (intentionally or not) to anger. For a good introduction to Ellis's thought, see *The Albert Ellis Reader: A*

Guide to Well-Being Using Rational Emotive Behavior Therapy, ed.
Albert Ellis and Shawn Blau (Secaucus, N.J.: Citadel Press/Carol
Publishing Group, 1998). See also Thurman, *The Lies We Believe,*
54-7.

22. Proverbs 19:11, NASB.

23. Adapted from Johann Christoph Arnold, *Why Forgive?* (Farming-
ton, Pa.: Plough Publishing, 2000), 33-4.

Chapter 3

1. Dorothy Sayers, "The Other Six Deadly Sins," in *The Whimsical
Christian* (New York: Macmillan/Collier Books, 1987), 176.

2. Proverbs 26:15, NLT.

3. G. K. Chesterton, *The Collected Works of G. K. Chesterton,* ed.
George Marlin (San Francisco: Ignatius, 1987), 4:61.

4. Jeremiah 30:21.

5. Mark Oppenheimer, "Salvation Without Sacrifice," *Charlotte
Observer,* 30 October 2000, sec. 11A.

6. See Henry Fairlie, *The Seven Deadly Sins Today* (Notre Dame, Ind.:
University of Notre Dame Press, 1978), 123.

7. Geoffrey Chaucer, "The Parson's Tale," in *The Canterbury Tales,* ed.
W. W. Skeat, sequence by Thomas Tyrwhitt, *Great Books of the
Western World,* ed. Robert Maynard Hutchins (Chicago: Ency-
clopaedia Britannica, 1952), 22:527.

8. Søren Kierkegaard, *A Kierkegaard Anthology,* ed. Robert Bretall (New York: Modern Library, 1959), 53.

9. For a good summation of the many stories and commentaries on the slaying of Kitty Genovese, now a universal symbol of Americans' failure to get involved, see Michael Dorman's "The Killing of Kitty Genovese" in Long Island: Our Story at http://www.lihistory.com.

10. Adapted from "Woman Dies After Cries for Help Ignored," *Charlotte Observer,* 27 May 1999, sec. 6A.

11. See James 1:22-24.

12. Vaclav Havel, *Letters to Olga: June 1979–September 1982,* trans. Paul Wilson (London: Faber and Faber, 1990), 235.

13. On this idea, see James Emery White, *Life-Defining Moments* (Colorado Springs, Colo.: WaterBrook, 2001).

14. Proverbs 20:4, TEV.

15. Adapted from William J. Bennett, ed., *The Book of Virtues* (New York: Simon & Schuster, 1993), 355.

16. Eugene Peterson, *The Contemplative Pastor: Returning to the Art of Spiritual Direction* (Grand Rapids, Mich.: Eerdmans, 1993), 19.

17. For this insight, I am indebted to Sayers, "The Other Six Deadly Sins," 176.

18. Robert MacNeil, "The Trouble with Television," *Reader's Digest,* March 1985, 171-4.

19. Proverbs 22:13, TLB.

20. Eric Reed, "Adversity and the Lesson of the Coffee Bean," *Leadership Journal*, found at http://www.PreachingToday.com.

21. Proverbs 10:4; 13:4, TLB.

22. See James C. Collins and Jerry I. Porras, *Built to Last: Successful Habits of Visionary Companies* (New York: HarperCollins, 1994).

23. Hebrews 12:1, TLB.

24. Jefferson to Martha, 1787, referenced in Dumas Malone, *Jefferson the Virginian* (Boston: Little, Brown, 1948), 1:56.

25. Ecclesiastes 9:10.

26. Adapted from Ted Engstrom, *The Fine Art of Friendship* (Nashville, Tenn.: Nelson, 1985), 31-2, which was adapted from Earl Nightingale's audiocassette series *Insight*.

27. 1 Corinthians 15:58.

28. Adapted from the national airing by NBC of the 1998 Hawaiian Open Ironman Triathlon, rebroadcast on 25 July 1999.

29. Philippians 4:13, NKJV. For information on Laura Wilkinson, see http://www.usadiving.org/bios/wilkinson.htm.

30. Adapted from *The Pastor's Weekly Briefing* 8, no. 39 (29 September 2000): 1.

31. See Fairlie, *The Seven Deadly Sins Today*, 129.

Chapter 4

1. Adapted from Charles Panati, *Extraordinary Origins of Everyday Things* (New York: Harper & Row, 1987), 85.

2. Eric Schlosser, *Fast Food Nation* (New York: Houghton Mifflin, 2001), 4.

3. Information on these products was gathered from Joanne Czarnecki with Shelley Drozd, "Rating the Fat Fighters," *Men's Health* (January/February 1999): 60-5.

4. *Men's Fitness* 13, no. 9 (September 1997): 42.

5. Greg Winter, "Weight-Loss Ads Driven by Desperation," *Charlotte Observer,* 29 October 2000, sec. 1A, 14A.

6. Information on NAAFA was taken from the official Web site at http://www.naafa.org/documents/brochures/naafa-info.html.

7. Nan Lyons, *Gluttony: More Is More,* vol. 1 of *The Sin Series* (New York: Red Rock Press, 1999), 15.

8. C. S. Lewis, *The Screwtape Letters,* rev. ed. (New York: Macmillan/Collier, 1982), 76.

9. See Matthew 4:2-4.

10. David Briscoe, "Many Remain Hungry, but Obesity Growing As Worldwide Food Worry," *Charlotte Observer,* 5 March 2000, sec. 7A.

11. Nanci Hellmich, "61% of Americans Overweight, Latest Health Survey Finds," *USA Today,* 15 December 2000, sec. 2A.

12. As cited by Dennis Okholm, "Rx for Gluttony," *Christianity Today* 44, no. 10, 4 September 2000, 63.

13. Barbara Crossette, "Ranks of 'Malnourished' Expand," *Charlotte Observer,* 17 January 2000, sec. 3A.

14. Roald Dahl, *Charlie and the Chocolate Factory* (New York: Knopf, 1964), 27.

15. Dahl, *Charlie and the Chocolate Factory,* 27.

16. For more on this, though you probably have had enough, see Lyons, *Gluttony,* 24. The best picture of Rome's gluttonous ways is the lavish banquets of Trimalchio in Petronius's *Satyricon.*

17. Adapted from Lyons, *Gluttony,* 44.

18. See Gerald G. May, *Addiction and Grace: Love and Spirituality in the Healing of Addictions* (New York: HarperSanFrancisco, 1991), 55. See also Henry Fairlie, *The Seven Deadly Sins Today* (Notre Dame, Ind.: University of Notre Dame Press, 1979), 166-7.

19. Dana Rosen-Perez, "Supermodel Turns Role Model: Urges Treatment for Eating Disorders," April 2000, Medscape, Inc., found at http://www.CBSHealthWatch.aol.com/aolmedscape.

20. See Os Guinness, *Steering Through Chaos: Vice and Virtue in an Age of Moral Confusion,* ed. Virginia Mooney (Colorado Springs, Colo.: NavPress, 2000), 214.

21. Frederick Buechner, *Telling Secrets* (New York: HarperCollins, 1991), 23.

22. John Eldredge, *The Journey of Desire* (Nashville, Tenn.: Nelson, 2000), 14.

23. Lewis, *The Screwtape Letters,* 79.

24. Humphrey Sydenham, *Sermons Upon Solemn Occasions* (n.p., 1637), 106, quoted in William Ian Miller, "Gluttony," in *Wicked Pleasures,* ed. Robert C. Solomon (Lanham, Md.: Rowman & Littlefield, 1999), 23.

25. Habakkuk was speaking specifically of wine, but the context applies it to all gods of the stomach; Habakkuk 2:5.

26. 1 Corinthians 6:19-20.

27. See Ephesians 5:18.

28. Miller, *Wicked Pleasures,* 43.

29. Romans 12:1.

30. Adapted from Tim Stafford, *That's Not What I Meant* (Grand Rapids, Mich.: Zondervan, 1995), 7-9.

31. 1 Peter 3:3-4, NLT.

32. Margery Williams, *The Velveteen Rabbit* (New York: Doubleday, 1958), 16-7.

33. Matthew 4:3.

34. Matthew 4:4.

35. John 4:32-34.

36. C. S. Lewis, "The Weight of Glory," in *The Weight of Glory and Other Essays,* rev. and exp. ed. (New York: Macmillan/Collier, 1980), 3-4.

Chapter 5

1. For the life of Mozart, see Don Campbell, *The Mozart Effect* (New York: Avon Books, 1997); Peter Gay, *Mozart,* in the Penguin Lives series, ed. James Atlas (New York: Lipper/Viking, 1999); Maynard Solomon, *Mozart: A Life* (New York: HarperCollins, 1995). On the film *Amadeus,* see Ken Gire, *Reflections on the Movies: Hearing God in the Unlikeliest of Places* (Colorado Springs, Colo.: Victor, 2000), 79-87. The film *Amadeus* was produced by Saul Zaentz and directed by Milos Forman. The screenplay was written by Peter Shaffer. It should be noted that Shaffer's screenplay is closer to legend than history, though rumors did swirl following Mozart's death that Salieri had poisoned him.

2. Herman Melville, quoted in Os Guinness, *Steering Through Chaos: Vice and Virtue in an Age of Moral Confusion,* ed. Virginia Mooney (Colorado Springs, Colo.: NavPress, 2000), 71.

3. Solomon Schimmel, *The Seven Deadly Sins* (Oxford, England: Oxford University Press, 1997), 57.

4. Cornelius Plantinga Jr., *Not the Way It's Supposed to Be* (Grand Rapids, Mich.: Eerdmans, 1995), 167.

5. Dante Alighieri, *The Divine Comedy of Dante Alighieri, Purgatory,* canto 13, trans. Charles Eliot Norton, vol. 21 of *Great Books of the*

Western World, ed. Robert Maynard Hutchins (Chicago: Encyclopaedia Britannica, 1952), 72-3.

6. See Maxie Dunnam and Kimberly Dunnam Reisman, *The Workbook on the Seven Deadly Sins* (Nashville, Tenn.: Upper Room Books, 1997), 52.

7. See Henry Fairlie, *The Seven Deadly Sins Today* (Notre Dame, Ind.: University of Notre Dame Press, 1978), 63-4.

8. Will D. Campbell, *Brother to a Dragonfly* (New York: Continuum, 1987), 181.

9. Aristotle, *Rhetoric,* bk. 2, sec. 10–11.

10. Romans 12:15.

11. Dorothy Sayers, "The Other Six Deadly Sins," in *The Whimsical Christian* (New York: Macmillan/Collier Books, 1987), 171.

12. Adapted from Hesketh Pearson, *Oscar Wilde: His Life and Wit* (New York: Harper & Brothers, 1946), 127-8.

13. See Plantinga, *Not the Way It's Supposed to Be,* 162.

14. Frederick Buechner, *Wishful Thinking: A Theological ABC* (New York: Harper & Row, 1973), 20.

15. Charles R. Swindoll, *Come Before Winter* (Portland, Oreg.: Multnomah, 1985), 98-9.

16. See Plantinga, *Not the Way It's Supposed to Be,* 169.

17. *Aucassin and Nicolette and Other Medieval Romances and Legends,* trans. Eugene Mason (London: J. M. Dent, 1910), 129-31. Also adapted from the retelling of Don Herzog, "Envy," in *Wicked Pleasures,* ed. Robert C. Solomon (Lanham, Md.: Rowman & Littlefield, 1999), 143.

18. Genesis 4.

19. James 3:14-16.

20. Angus Wilson, "Envy," in *The Seven Deadly Sins,* ed. Ian Fleming (New York: William Morrow, 1962), 11.

21. See Tony Campolo, *Seven Deadly Sins* (Wheaton, Ill.: Victor, 1987), 106.

22. Adapted from Jerry Newcombe and Kristi Newcombe, *A Way of Escape: Experiencing God's Victory Over Temptation* (Nashville, Tenn.: Broadman & Holman, 1999), 74.

23. Adapted from *Aesop Without Morals,* trans. and ed. Lloyd W. Daly (New York: Thomas Yoseloff, 1961), 205, in Herzog, "Envy," 150.

24. Adapted from Harry S. Stout, *The Divine Dramatist: George Whitefield and the Rise of Modern Evangelicalism* (Grand Rapids, Mich.: Eerdmans, 1991), 201; Charles R. Swindoll, *Dropping Your Guard: The Value of Open Relationships* (Waco, Tex.: Word, 1983), 73; and Leslie B. Flynn, *Great Church Fights* (Wheaton, Ill.: Victor, 1976), 44.

25. See Fairlie, *The Seven Deadly Sins Today,* 80. See also Geoffrey Chaucer, "The Parson's Tale," *The Canterbury Tales,* ed. W. W.

Skeat, sequence by Thomas Tyrwhitt, vol. 22 of *The Great Books of the Western World,* ed. Robert Maynard Hutchins (Chicago: Encyclopaedia Britannica, 1952), 518; and Alighieri, *The Divine Comedy,* canto 13, 2.

26. Psalm 73:21-22, MSG.

27. Psalm 73:23-24, MSG.

28. Psalm 73:25,28, MSG.

29. As cited by Billy Graham, *Hope for the Troubled Heart* (Dallas, Tex.: Word, 1991), 44-5.

30. Psalm 73:25,28, MSG.

Chapter 6

1. A number of sources were used to compile this overview of the eighties, but of invaluable assistance was Bernard Grun's *The Timetables of History,* 3d ed. (New York: Touchstone, 1991). A debt is also owed to Bill Hybels for a small turn of the phrase at the end of the paragraph, stolen boldly from his sermon series titled "Signs of the Times."

2. As reported by Susan Trausch, "Down to the Raw Nerve," *Boston Globe,* 30 January 1991, 15. See also Solomon Schimmel, *The Seven Deadly Sins* (Oxford, England: Oxford University Press, 1997), 3.

3. As reported by Dyan Machan, "An Edison for a New Age," *Forbes,* 17 May 1999, 181.

4. As reported by Geoff Cook, "Hey, I Just Work Here," *Wired,* March 2000, 232. Both this quote and the aforementioned woman at Priceline.com were brought to my attention by Dinesh D'Souza in his book *The Virtue of Prosperity: Finding Values in an Age of Techno-Affluence* (New York: The Free Press, 2000), 6.

5. Rob Walker, "But Will It Buy Happiness?" *New York Times Book Review,* 3 January 2001, 12.

6. *Fast Company,* July/August 1999, 112. The specific question was "If you could have one more hour per day at home or one of the following, which would you rather have?" In the pairing "a $10,000 a year raise" vs. "one more hour per day at home," 83 percent chose the raise, and 17 percent selected the time.

7. Mitch Albom, *Tuesdays with Morrie* (New York: Doubleday, 1997), 124.

8. Henry Fairlie, *The Seven Deadly Sins Today* (Notre Dame, Ind.: University of Notre Dame Press, 1978), 135.

9. Luke 12:15-21.

10. Beyond Jesus' words, we find greed denounced in the tenth commandment. The apostle Paul in 1 Timothy 6:10 bluntly says that the love of money is the root of all evil.

11. Michael Lewis, *The New New Thing: A Silicon Valley Story* (New York: Norton, 2000), 260.

12. See Luke 12:20.

13. Leo Tolstoy, "How Much Land Does a Man Need?" (n.p., 1886), trans. Louis Maude and Aylmer Maude, quoted in Os Guinness, *Steering Through Chaos: Vice and Virtue in an Age of Moral Confusion,* ed. Virginia Mooney (Colorado Springs, Colo.: NavPress, 2000), 182-97.

14. See Matthew 6:24.

15. Frederick Buechner, *Whistling in the Dark* (New York: Harper & Row, 1988), 80.

16. Matthew 6:21, NLT.

17. Proverbs 23:7, NKJV.

18. James Patterson and Peter Kim, *The Day America Told the Truth* (New York: Prentice Hall, 1991), 65.

19. Robert Todd Carroll, quoted in Drew Fetherston, *Greed and Its Rewards,* vol. 3 of *The Sin Series* (New York: Red Rock Press, 2000), 108.

20. C. S. Lewis, *The Voyage of the Dawn Treader* (New York: Collier/Macmillan, 1970), 75.

21. Tony Campolo, *Seven Deadly Sins* (Wheaton, Ill.: Victor, 1987), 144-5. Used by permission of the author.

22. Luke 12:20.

23. Adapted from Carey Goldberg, "Real-Space Meetings Fill in the Cyberspace Gaps," *New York Times,* 25 February 1997, sec. A8.

24. Luke 12:15.

25. Luke 6:38.

26. Proverbs 28:27.

27. 2 Corinthians 9:6.

28. "The New Philanthropy," *Time*, 24 July 2000.

Chapter 7

1. Eric Tisdale, "My Girlfriend's Father—What a Man!" *Glamour*, June 1998, quoted in Wendy Shalit, *A Return to Modesty* (New York: The Free Press, 1999), 194.

2. See J. Allan Petersen, *The Myth of the Greener Grass*, rev. ed. (Wheaton, Ill.: Tyndale, 1991).

3. Lynn Elber, "Study Finds TV More Sexual," *Charlotte Observer*, 7 February 2001, sec. 4A.

4. Adapted from Eve Baguedor, "Is Anyone Faithful Anymore?" *McCall's*, February 1973, 73.

5. C. S. Lewis, *Mere Christianity* (New York: Macmillan, 1952), 75.

6. Proverbs 23:7, NKJV.

7. Adapted from Charles R. Swindoll, *Laugh Again* (Dallas, Tex.: Word, 1991), 12.

8. Genesis 2:18,22,24-25.

9. Proverbs 5:18-19, TLB.

10. Song of Songs 1:2-3.

11. Song of Songs 1:13.

12. Song of Songs 1:15-16, TLB.

13. 1 Corinthians 6:16, MSG.

14. Adapted from Tony Campolo, *Seven Deadly Sins* (Wheaton, Ill.: Victor, 1987), 52.

15. As noted by Maxie Dunnam and Kimberly Dunnam Reisman, *The Workbook on the Seven Deadly Sins* (Nashville, Tenn.: Upper Room Books, 1997), 141.

16. As an example, see the repeated warnings throughout chapters 5, 6, and 7 of the book of Proverbs.

17. Bill Hybels and Rob Wilkins, *Tender Love* (Chicago: Moody Press, 1993), 38.

18. 1 Corinthians 6:13.

19. Clarence Page, "Remembering the Big Dipper's Other Statistics," *Chicago Tribune,* 17 October 1999. Found at preachingtoday.com.

20. "We've Got Porn," *Christianity Today* 44, no. 7, 12 June 2000, 32. Found at http://www.christianitytoday.com/ct/2000/007/29.32.html.

21. Timothy Egan, "$10 Billion Porn Industry Entices Major Companies," *Charlotte Observer,* 23 October 2000, sec. 5A.

22. Hebrews 13:4, MSG.

23. Tamar Lewin, "What Is 'Sex'? To Teens, Some Acts Don't Count," *Charlotte Observer,* 19 December 2000, sec. 3A.

24. For more on this, see James Emery White, *You Can Experience an Authentic Life* (Nashville, Tenn.: Word, 2000).

25. 1 Corinthians 6:17-18, MSG.

26. "Adultery: A New Furor over an Old Sin," *Newsweek,* 30 September 1996, 56.

27. See Linda Waite and Maggie Gallaher, *The Case for Marriage* (New York: Doubleday, 2000). See also Judith S. Wallerstein, Julia M. Lewis, and Sandra Blakeslee, *The Unexpected Legacy of Divorce: A 25-Year Landmark Study* (New York: Hyperion, 2000).

28. 1 Corinthians 6:18-19, MSG.

29. Proverbs 6:27-28,32, MSG.

30. Adapted from Erica Goode, "With Fears Fading, More Gays Spurn Old Preventive Message," 19 August 2001, *New York Times.* Found at http://www.nytimes.com/2001/08/19/health/19RISK.

31. Louis McBurney, M.D., *Leadership Journal* 6, no. 3 (summer 1985).

32. Owen Chadwick, ed., *Western Asceticism,* Library of Christian Classics, Ichthus ed. (Philadelphia: Westminster, 1958), 69.

33. Solomon Schimmel, *The Seven Deadly Sins* (Oxford, England: Oxford University Press, 1997), 118.

34. Genesis 39:9.

35. "www.pornsite.com Pulling Megaprofits," *Current Thoughts and Trends,* August 2000, 25, adapted from Brendan Koerner, "A Lust for Profits," *U.S. News and World Report* 128, no. 12 (27 March 2000): 36-8.

36. Gary Webb, "Sex and the Internet: A Special Report," *Yahoo! Internet Life* 7, no. 5 (May 2001): 90.

37. Proverbs 5:21, NLT.

38. Chadwick, *Western Asceticism,* 62.

39. Adapted from Randy Alcorn, "Strategies to Keep from Falling," *Leadership Journal* 17, no. 3 (summer 1996): 49.

40. See 2 Corinthians 10:5.

41. Adapted from Edward K. Rowell, ed., *Fresh Illustrations for Preaching and Teaching from Leadership Journal* (Grand Rapids, Mich.: Baker, 1997), 150.

Chapter 8

1. Adapted from "A Tale of Two Reggies," *Parade Magazine,* 7 January 2001, 6.

2. C. S. Lewis, *Mere Christianity* (New York: Macmillan, 1952), 94.

3. Cornelius Plantinga Jr., *Not the Way It's Supposed to Be* (Grand Rapids, Mich.: Eerdmans, 1995), 84.

4. Dorothy Sayers, "The Other Six Deadly Sins," in *The Whimsical Christian* (New York: Macmillan/Collier Books, 1987), 177.

5. Dante Alighieri, *The Divine Comedy of Dante Alighieri,* trans. Charles Eliot Norton, vol. 21 of *Great Books of the Western World,* ed. Robert Maynard Hutchins (Chicago: Encyclopaedia Britannica, 1952), 68.

6. Henry Fairlie, *The Seven Deadly Sins Today* (Notre Dame, Ind.: University of Notre Dame Press, 1978), 41.

7. Sayers, "The Other Six Deadly Sins," 177-9.

8. Ezekiel 28:2.

9. Bertrand Russell, *Power, A New Social Analysis* (New York: Norton, 1969), 11.

10. Isaiah 14:12-14.

11. Ezekiel 28:17.

12. This idea has been set forth by many, including Lewis in *Mere Christianity,* 96.

13. John Milton, *Paradise Lost,* in *The Complete Poetical Works of John Milton,* ed. Douglas Bush (Boston: Houghton Mifflin, 1965), 218.

14. See Lewis, *Mere Christianity,* 94.

15. 2 Chronicles 26:5.

16. 2 Chronicles 26:20.

17. 2 Chronicles 26:16. See also Proverbs 16:18.

18. Plantinga, *Not the Way It's Supposed to Be*, 82.

19. Christopher Lasch, *The Culture of Narcissism* (New York: Norton, 1978).

20. John Calvin, *Institutes*, vol. 1, trans. Henry Beveridge (Grand Rapids, Mich.: Eerdmans, 1983), 2.2.11.

21. Augustine, *The City of God, Nicene and Post-Nicene Fathers*, vol. 2, ed. Philip Schaff (1887; reprint, Peabody, Mass.: Hendrickson Publishers, 1999), 14.13, citing the apocryphal work *The Wisdom of Jesus the Son of Sirach* and quoting Ecclesiasticus 10:15.

22. Romans 12:3.

23. Adapted from two sources: Stephen R. Covey, *The Seven Habits of Highly Effective People* (New York: Simon & Schuster, 1989), 33, which cited Frank Koch in *Proceedings*, the magazine of the Naval Institute; also Craig Brian Larson, ed., *Illustrations from Leadership Journal* (Grand Rapids, Mich.: Baker, 1993), 134.

24. See C. S. Lewis, *The Screwtape Letters*, rev. ed. (New York: Macmillan/Collier, 1982), 64.

25. Fairlie, *The Seven Deadly Sins Today*, 57.

26. Adapted from Philip Yancey, *Reaching for the Invisible God* (Grand Rapids, Mich.: Zondervan, 2000), 163.

27. Erving Goffman, as cited in Tony Campolo, *Seven Deadly Sins* (Wheaton, Ill.: Victor, 1987), 82-3.

28. Robert F. Morneau, *Humility*, as found at www.christianitytoday.com/ct/2000/009/26.68.html.

29. Calvin, *Institutes*, 2.2.11.

30. As cited in a display in the Visitor's Center of The Cove, the Billy Graham Training Center in Asheville, North Carolina.

31. 1 Corinthians 4:6-7.

32. See Matthew 11:11.

33. John 3:30.

34. Jeremiah 45:5.

35. Jim Collins, *Good to Great* (New York: HarperBusiness, 2001), 21. Emphasized words are original with the author.

36. Lewis, *Mere Christianity*, 99.

37. Adapted from Hans Christian Anderson, "The Teapot," trans. Kirsti Saebo Newcombe, in *The Moral of the Story*, comp. and ed. Jerry Newcombe (Nashville, Tenn.: Broadman & Holman, 1996), 118-20.

Chapter 9

1. C. S. Lewis, *Surprised by Joy: The Shape of My Early Life* (London: G Bles, 1955; New York: Harcourt, Brace, 1956).

2. Luke 2:10-11.

3. John R. W. Stott, *Authentic Christianity* (Downers Grove, Ill.: Inter-Varsity, 1995), 222.

4. Millard Erickson, *Concise Dictionary* (Grand Rapids, Mich.: Baker, 1986), 89.

5. John Cassian, *The Monastic Institutes: Consisting of "On the Training of a Monk" and "The Eight Deadly Sins": In Twelve Books,* book 5, trans. Jerome Bertram (London: Saint Austin Press, 1999), 69.

6. Cassian, *Institutes,* book 9, 140.

7. Cassian, *Institutes,* book 9, 140.

8. Cassian, *Institutes,* book 10, 145.

9. Claire Soares, "Health Experts Vow to Fight Depression Stigma," Reuters News Agency, 6 April 2001, found at America Online.

10. David Ho, "More Report Being Close to 'Breakdown,'" *Charlotte Observer,* 3 July 2000, sec. 3A.

11. For information on Luther and Spurgeon, see Dwight L. Carlson, "Exposing the Myth that Christians Should Not Have Emotional Problems," *Christianity Today* 42, no. 2 (9 February 1998): 28.

12. Samuel H. Chao, "Remarkable or Little-Known Facts About Hudson Taylor and Missions to China," *Christian History* 15, no. 4 (fall 1996): 2.

13. Carlson, "Exposing the Myth," 28.

14. Beyond depression, or more accurately major depressive disorder, there is dysthymia, bipolar disorder, and cyclothymia.

15. Carlson, "Exposing the Myth," 28.

16. Larry Crabb, *Connecting* (Nashville, Tenn.: Word, 1997), 24.

17. Crabb, *Connecting*, 26-7. For a breakdown of what might be considered physical and what might be considered spiritual, see pages 203-7. A thorough diagnosis would also seek to rule out positive answers caused by premenstrual syndrome, thyroid imbalance, low blood sugar, anemia, and seasonal affective disorder.

18. For information on Vincent van Gogh's life, particularly the religious dimensions, see Kathleen Powers Erickson, *At Eternity's Gate: The Spiritual Vision of Vincent van Gogh* (Grand Rapids, Mich.: Eerdmans, 1998). It should be noted that while van Gogh's willful despair at the earlier developments is without question, biographers are mixed as to the cause of his eventual suicide.

19. See 1 Kings 18:16-40, author's paraphrase.

20. 1 Kings 18:27-29.

21. 1 Kings 18:36-39.

22. 1 Kings 19:3-5.

23. 1 Kings 19:5-8.

24. See Matthew 4.

25. Psalm 127:2.

26. Martin Moore-Ede, *The Twenty-Four Hour Society* (Reading, Mass.: Addison-Wesley, 1993).

27. 1 Kings 19:11-12.

28. L. B. Cowman, *Springs in the Valley* (Grand Rapids, Mich.: Zondervan, 1939).

29. Psalm 46:10, NCV.

30. James 4:8.

31. This observation, as well as the dialogue from the movie *Nell,* are taken from Ken Gire, *The Reflective Life* (Colorado Springs, Colo.: Chariot Victor, 1998), 9-11. See also Mary Ann Evans, *Nell* (New York: Berkley Books, 1995), 242-3.

32. 1 Kings 19:15-17.

A Final Word

1. Sebastian Junger, *The Perfect Storm* (New York: Norton, 1997).

2. Adapted from Lee Strobel, *The Case for Faith* (Grand Rapids, Mich.: Zondervan, 2000), 256-9, as well as Strobel's retelling of it in "Meet the Jesus I Know," *Preaching Today,* tape 211, published by Christianity Today International, Carol Stream, Illinois. Material adapted from *The Case for Faith.* Used by permission of Zondervan, Grand Rapids, Michigan.

About the Author

James Emery White is the founding and senior pastor of Mecklenburg Community Church in Charlotte, North Carolina. Dr. White holds an M.Div. and a Ph.D. degree from Southern Seminary and has completed advanced graduate study at Vanderbilt University and postdoctoral continuing education at the University of Oxford, England. His previous books include *Rethinking the Church, A Search for the Spiritual,* and *Life-Defining Moments.* He and his wife, Susan, live in Charlotte with their four children, Rebecca, Rachel, Jonathan, and Zachary.

To learn more about WaterBrook Press and view
our catalog of products, log on to our Web site:
www.waterbrookpress.com

WATERBROOK
PRESS